The Christian Faith
and the
Marxist Criticism of Religion

The Christian Faith
and the
Marxist Criticism of Religion

Helmut Gollwitzer

Charles Scribner's Sons · New York

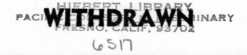

This book was originally published in German under
the title "Die marxistische Religionskritik und der
christliche Glaube" in *Marxismusstudien,* 7th Series,
© 1962 by J. C. B. Mohr (Paul Siebeck), Tübingen, Germany.

© The Saint Andrew Press 1970

Translated into the English language by David Cairns

Printed in Great Britain.
Library of Congress Catalog Card Number 69-17055

CONTENTS

A*

Preface to the English Edition

TEN years after the composition of this work and six years after its first publication the English edition appears in a profoundly changed situation. In the group in which its contents were first read—the Commission on Marxism of the Study Fellowship of the Evangelical Academies in Germany —there was not one committed Marxist to be found. In that group one was dealing with Marxism on a high level but without Marxists, and this was not the fault of the group. The West German Marxists, the Leninist wing of which on account of the ban on the Communist party had been driven underground, had no interest in informal conversation with non-Marxists who were interested. From time to time the Commission had guests from non-German Communist parties associated with it; yet it was symptomatic that at both meetings concerned with Christian-Marxist relations no Marxist was present. On the Christian side there were not a few who wished to have a dialogue with Marxists, but this desire was not echoed on the Marxist side, either because they were busy with more actual problems or because they held to the principle that religion was something which had already been disposed of, so that a dialogue with its representatives did not seem to be worth while.

With the progress of de-Stalinization, there has been a fundamental change in this respect. In Western Europe, in Czecho-Slovakia (thanks to the preparatory work there of Josef L. Hromadka and his circle), in North and South America, though unfortunately not yet in the Soviet Union,

Marxists, including official representatives of the Communist party, have entered into the dialogue, and taken a lively interest in it. I regret that my book came too early to benefit from the fruits of this discussion.

Another change in the situation is connected with this. Today the youth of Europe and America have been seized by a profound unrest which gives rise to great hopes. They have a vivid sense of the coercion and exploitation which characterizes both the social system of the West and that of the East, and in their social criticism they make use of the instrument of Marxist analysis. Here the hitherto scholastic Marxism of the Communist party has been resolved into a supple, truly critical and dialectical thinking, which has gained a new vision of the humane Utopia, and presses for the abandonment of the rigid structures of domination in the West as in the East. This neo-Marxism of the young generation is different from the traditional Marxism in essential points. The young generation have no interest in the monolithic character of the party, and in the emphasis placed on party-unity by the creation of a universal world-view as a substitute for religion, after the manner of the Marxism of Friedrich Engels. The anti-religious prejudice of traditional Marxism is not found among them, indeed, they are asking expectantly for a new Christianity which will take seriously the dynamic and humanitarian content of the biblical message, with its criticism of society, to which Marxist thinkers like Ernst Bloch have drawn their attention. This frees Socialist thinking from the discredit cast upon it by Stalinism, and the questions addressed to Christian theology, which are contained in Marxism, gain a new actuality. Christian theology must face the responsibility of listening to these questions and dealing with them.

The following criticisms have been made of my discussion:
1. It pays too little attention to the differences between the individual forms of Marxism, especially the difference

between Karl Marx and his successors, beginning with Engels, and

2. It pays too little attention to the social conditioning of Marxist atheism, so that in my pages the latter appears too much as an isolated world-view like that of L. Feuerbach. I have mentioned both these criticisms, but believe that the way in which I have discussed the matter is justified and useful, because the assertion of the world-view that religion is out of date and harmful was common to all representatives of traditional Marxism, and consequently cannot be left out of account in the new dialogue. The limitation of my book is deliberate, and must certainly not be overlooked.

There is another point which should not be disregarded; my criticism of the Messianism in the Marxist tradition is not a plea for Reformism. It should help to make clear the distinction between (1) the promise of the Kingdom of God, (2) the Utopia of a successful earthly society, and (3) a concrete socio-political programme, a distinction which will prevent Marxism from offering itself as a substitute for religion. But my criticism of Messianism does not seek to unmask the social Utopia as an empty dream, or reduce the revolutionary impulse to a resigned trade unionism. Recently, when Berlin students invited me to summarize my book for them in the form of a lecture, I found myself, to their astonishment, compelled to put the accent in a different place. I did not speak about the arrogance of Messianism as a harmful element in Marxism, but about the responsibility of Christians for such a social Utopia as their proclamation of the Kingdom of God and the commandment to love our neighbour makes obligatory upon them. In this universal context, and only in it, has this book its place.

Berlin, 1 July 1968.   HELMUT GOLLWITZER

Introduction

THIS essay is the enlarged version of a paper which I gave at two sittings of the Marxism-Commission on 2 October 1958, and on 3 March 1959. It removes as far as possible the study of the Marxist attitude to religion from its historical and philosophical context, in order thus to make it possible to bring together within limited compass the essential sources and discuss them. The material belonging to natural philosophy was removed, because there is a considerable amount of literature dealing with it, and because, in my opinion, it becomes inessential if the questions dealt with here are clarified.

The essay may be understood as a contribution to the Christian-Marxist dialogue. It was written in inner and outer contact with those who through their situation in life are continually involved in this dialogue. The dialogue compels us to leave the quiet aloofness in which the historian sees a historical movement as a unity whose essential elements are necessarily and indissolubly linked. What the dialogue seeks to accomplish is the dissolution of these connections. Their necessity, because it has a historical character, must be regarded as merely relative, since, like history itself, it is still open to the future and undecided. I underline this under the impression which the historical study of the origins of modern political Messianism has made upon me, as contained in J. L. Talmon's *Die Ursprung der totalitären Demokratie.*[1] With the exception of the chapter on Jacobinism, printed in *Der Monat* of March 1952, I did not read this book till after

[1] Cologne, 1961.

the completion of my essay. Talmon's terminology coincides in part with my own.

It will be observed that in this essay the use of terms varies. Sometimes I speak of "Marxism", sometimes of "Communism". The reason for this is that there are no clearly marked boundaries between the different schools of thought which stem from Marx. None the less, as far as possible, I have made this distinction, that by "Marxism-Leninism", I describe the official doctrine of the parties which stand under Soviet leadership, by "Communism" I mean the movement, which, including its Titoist and Trotskyite variations, was stamped with the mark of Lenin; and by "Marxism" I mean the original doctrine created by Marx and Engels, in which also non-Communists today participate, in so far as Marx is not merely one influence among others upon them.

This study is dedicated to Professor Fritz Lieb of Basle on his seventieth birthday on 10 June 1962—a man who has taken part in the above-mentioned dialogue, with an intensity and knowledge that few others could parallel, and has made important contributions to it, as the bibliography of his collected essays dealing with it shows.[2] The present author cannot imagine what his own career would have been like without the impetus which he received from Fritz Lieb's impassioned instruction, since his time as a student at Bonn in the last Semesters before the "Extirpation of Marxism" which was undertaken in 1933. The Marxism Commission also owes its gratitude to him for his continuing co-operation.

[2] F. Lieb, *Sophia und Historie*, Zürich, 1962.

CHAPTER ONE

The Significance of the Theme

WE are confronted by the phenomenon of Marxism's decisive repudiation of everything which can conceivably be included under the title of "religion". The character and consequences of this repudiation, its motives and arguments, will have to be expounded and tested. But the phenomenon itself, to start with, is sufficiently striking. It is a consistent characteristic of all the developmental phases of Communism from that of the early Marx, through Engels and Lenin right down to post-Stalinian Communism. Here the party orthodoxy of the Soviets is at one with the deviationism of the Trotskyites and the followers of Tito. However great the changes which "creative further development" may have introduced into the original doctrine—on this point the verdict has remained sharply negative. However much occasion political tactics may have given for alliance with religious groups, and for the soft-pedalling of anti-religious agitation, this repudiation was never renounced or even concealed. If any Marxist changed, or even weakened, on this issue, that was the clearest sign that he was either beginning to move away from Marxism, or had already done so. Or else it was a moderation and self-limitation of Marxism, indicating that it was no longer a *Weltanschauung* in the modern sense of the word—no longer an all-embracing outlook on the world and existence in all its aspects, which could guide a man's whole way of life, no longer an exhaustive answer to the fundamental questions of human life.[1]

---

[1] What Marxism as a world-outlook means by *Weltanschauung*, has been well formulated by the French Communist Jean-Richard

It is its verdict in the matter of religion which distinguishes Marxism as a genuine ideology, Marxism understood as a *Weltanschauung* from Marxism employed merely as a method. The man who has been converted to Marxist atheism has become a total convert, he regards Marxism as something to which one can be converted, to which one can dedicate one's total existence. The decision made at this point will have its effect in every sphere, both in a man's whole conception of Marxism and in his whole personality. If Communism—and I use this word as Marxists and Leninists understand it—were some day to change in this respect, then that would be an expression of the profoundest change in it.

1. Thus I believe that here we confront the very heart of all the problems relating to contemporary Communism. It is possible to object that the theologian who holds such an opinion overestimates the importance of the questions which are his special field of interest. It is precisely the Marxist who will remind us that Marx himself did not consider the criticism of religion a matter of central importance, but that it was precisely his concern to regard it as merely peripheral; he was convinced that it had been, in principle, completed, and that this end had been achieved by interpreting it not as of the first, but merely of the second rank of importance, and that by disclosing that religion is a symptom, and not the heart of human life. But this assertion is only an extreme formulation of the *claim* of Marxism; for by asserting the

---

Bloch. "Wherever we encounter man, that strange animal, whatever may be the colour of his skin, whatever the latitude and the climate, we shall find him occupied, in spite of contrary appearances, I may say, by one single thought, obsessed by one task and one unique passion; through all the accidents of life he asks the fundamental question of his destiny: 'What kind of being am I? What am I doing on the earth? What is my *raison d'être*? How can I explain this incessant activity in which I am engaged? How can I justify these desires which stir me, these anxieties which gnaw me?' In a word who will give me a definition of myself which can give me clarity, peace, and contentment?" (*Commune,* Paris, 1928, p. 423, quoted F. Mauriac and others, *Le Communisme et les Chrétiens,* Paris, 1937, pp. 11f.).

secondary character of religion it claims itself to be the fulfilment of man's primary interests. And thus even its denial of the central position of religion is an acknowledgment of the central significance of this question. But it cannot give a more emphatic expression to its own promise than by promising to make religion superfluous; it cannot say more clearly that it is concerned to "say good-bye to all previous history". For thus it promises to give a better answer to man's ultimate questions, his question concerning his origin and goal and destiny, the questions posed by the tragic character of human existence, by guilt and by death, and therefore an answer to the questions concerning his true duty, his real happiness; in a word concerning the meaning of human life—a better answer than could be found in the world of religion, even if this better answer were found to consist in the removal of the very causes of such questions.

Certainly this is the point where Marxism will find it hardest to prove its case. The fulfilment of this promise will cost it much more labour than its claim to replace capitalism by a better economic and social order. And this is one reason why in the regions where the Communist domination is most firmly established, religion is the only expression of "objective spirit' which still exists, which could neither be eliminated nor assimilated.

2. But we can see the significance of our theme also in the fact that it involves a debate with the whole trend of the modern spirit. The claim that the age of religion was past, that the time for its replacement by reason had come—this was not an assertion invented by Marxism, but one which had been inherited by it, and which had been proclaimed in various forms by the English deists down to Comte. If the hallmark of the Enlightenment was its certainty that the consistent use of rational and scientific methods had enabled it to enter upon a better and more dependable pathway to truth, freedom, and humanity, Marxism provides us with the most determined expression of the Enlightenment.

"Enlightenment" is here historically understood as the first high-water mark in the self-realization of the modern spirit.

It enters into conflict with Christianity, at least with the forms which the latter has hitherto taken. The shock-troops of the Enlightenment understand this as conflict with Christianity in general, which must be brought to trial. Revelation and reason, faith and knowledge, the sacred and the profane, are at odds, and the struggle about their right relationship is the still undecided theme of intellectual discussion today, which is closely intertwined with the dispute about the norms of social order.

It is just this intricate interconnection which Marxism has underlined in "Historical Materialism"; admittedly the scheme of relationships expounded in this system does not give clear expression to the fact that the various positions taken up in the intellectual dispute are not merely concealed forms of the class-struggle, but that the assertion of the claims of the individual in society is at stake, and the maintenance of the tension between the individual and society, of which we shall have to speak later, and whose defence must on no account be denounced as anti-social individualism. While this antithesis is described, though in a very provisional and unsatisfactory manner, as one between irrationalism and rationalism, we must never overlook the fact that *both positions* can become bastions of freedom in the struggle against the forces threatening it. Whether, and how far, they *are* so, is to be decided by consideration of the whole historical and political context, primarily by the context which the individual representative of such a position gives to his theory by the rest of his social and political action. The manner in which an individual and a group asserts the place of individual freedom within the framework of a social order, gives orientation and correction to his doctrine of the prospects of reason and his teaching about its limits. The slanders which each side hurls at the other must not blind us. It is not inevitable that rationalism should degenerate into

Jacobinical tyranny, nor is it any more inevitable that irrationalism should be the threshold of Fascism. Therefore to use both concepts, rationalism and irrationalism, as if they were mere labels, is to fall back to an earlier stage of the discussion, the stage of the Enlightenment as a historical epoch.[2]

Thus Marxist atheism cannot be judged in isolation, as if it were the accidental invention of a few especially irreverent and irreligious men. It may well be the case that Marxism is right in claiming that in itself the consistent content of modern thought comes to light, at least this cannot be denied out of hand; and in any case, in making its claim, Marxism can appeal to the powerful stream of rationalism in modern times, without which the evolution of such a thing as modern science is unthinkable. It is this rationalistic tradition which Marxism takes in earnest. In practice, Marxism is rationalism taken in earnest, a rationalism which refuses to be relativized and called in question by its provisionally continuing co-existence with other outlooks. Herein lies its difference to the easygoing tolerance with which middle-class atheism treats religion, and for this reason it shocks Christians who have long become accustomed to this easy-going tolerance, and seems to them particularly vicious, when they should be realizing that at last in Marxism, as in atheism, Christian faith has again an opponent which takes itself—and therefore also takes the faith seriously.[3]

[2] The adherence of G. Lukacs to this Procrustean schema (e.g. *Die Zerstörung der Vernunft*, Berlin, 1955), brings all his analyses under a dogmatic prejudice, to which he himself eventually fell a victim—the victim of an irrationalism which must necessarily be operative where the authority of reason is localized in an institution—as happens in the Leninist doctrine of the party.

[3] K. Barth, "Die Theologie und der heutige Mensch" in *Zwischen den Zeiten, Munich*, 1930, p. 387: "The repudiation of theology can signify a very genuine and necessary protest against theologians who have forgotten that the affirmation of theology is an act of war against a forcible, angry, and extremely understandable 'No' which protests against theologians who think they can have theology on all too easy terms. . . . Perhaps it was for just this purpose that these

5

In the debate with Marxism every man determines his own relation to the stream of intellectual life of our epoch, whether he co-operates with, and helps to determine its direction, or floats like a piece of driftwood with the current, whether he clings nervously to the bank, and is left behind, or is left high and dry, like the relic of an earlier flood, or belongs to the *avant garde* that has already left the present stage behind it. No human institution has been entrusted with the objective answer to these questions, although many behave as if this were the case, but everyone must know that, in defining his attitude, he must face these questions, and must reveal at least what his subjective intention is. It is the significance of Marxism that it belongs to those realities of our time which we cannot ignore without penalty in determining our own position. It is neither possible to make up one's mind about it without at the same time making up one's mind about the leading motifs of modern intellectual life, nor can we take up our own position in this realm without facing up to Marxism. Perhaps the day is near when Marxism will be a thing of past history, but that day has not yet dawned. Since there are among us not a few who as Christians have reacted to this encounter with violent hostility—one thinks of Catholic and Protestant Conservatism of the nineteenth century, and the later Hugo Ball and the early Gogarten[4]—it is not superfluous

---

resolute opponents of theology were given to him (the theologian); for this purpose were sent a Strauss and a Feuerbach, for this purpose a Nietzsche and an Overbeck, for this purpose, lastly, even the foolish clamour of the vulgar free-thinkers. If theologians know what theology is about, then they will find that, for example, there is much more realism in the wild rebellion against theology in Soviet Russia today than in the lukewarm toleration which it enjoys among us, or in the euthanasia, the peaceful blood-letting in North America which the polite godlessness of what is there termed 'Humanism' is trying to inflict upon all theology, in such fashion that theology itself is quite unaware of what is happening."

[4] Among the contemporary critics of Marxism in this connection, special mention must be made of the Catholic philosopher J. Hommes, *Der technische Eros. Das Wesen der materialistischen Geschichts-auffassung*, Freiburg, 1955.

to insist that it must be faced with a critical and open mind, and that even when Marxism is contradicted, we must never forget that the Marxists and we inherit common presuppositions and are summoned by common problems.

3. The consciousness of the opposition between Marxism and religion, or Christianity, as it is expressed by both sides, has up to this point been taken for granted by us. But the opposition is itself a problem. In assuming it, we operate with fixed magnitudes. But it is a very open question whether they are this. The Marxist may be certain that in his criticism of religion he has also said what was necessary about the Christian faith. But it is a very open question whether the Christian faith falls within the field of phenomena which are here described as religion, and what it has to do with this field of phenomena. So the attack of Marxism compels us to reflect on the particular character of Christianity. But while the latter loses the appearance of familiarity which can be taken for granted, the Christian attitude also to Marxism is not something fixed which can be taken for granted from the start, nor is it a logical and practical answer to that attack. We cannot automatically conclude from the Marxist view of Christianity how the Christian is to look upon Marxism. This is the reason why all theological representations of our theme at once imply positions taken up in the debate within the churches on the Christian attitude to Communism.[5] Communism, as the most massive anti-religious force, with the openly avowed goal of making Christianity an affair of the past,

[5] See on this point the discussion about W. H. Dirks' essay in *Frankfurter Hefte*, February 1947, on which Dirks has expressed himself in his rejoinder "*Die Frankfurter Hefte und der Marxismus*" op. cit., April 1952. See also the opposition between the works of M. Reding, especially *Der politische Atheismus*, Graz, 1957; "Marxismus and Atheismus" in *Marxismus-Leninismus, Geschichte und Gestalt*, Berlin, 1961, p. 160f., and those of J. Hommes (in addition to the book mentioned in the previous note), cf. *Koexistenz—philosophisch beleuchtet*, Bonn, 1957. On the Protestant side see the publications of J. L. Hromadka, J. Hamel, H. Thielicke, and E. Brunner.

poses for the Christian two questions which touch the heart of Christian existence today.

(a) Is it possible that here there becomes manifest what for long has been latently the authentic opinion of the age? Is Marxism the legitimate harvest of a seed which was sown long since? When did this sowing begin? In the nineteenth century, or in the eighteenth? Or in the Renaissance? Or as early as that rationalistic movement in which Christianity, in the days of late antiquity, allied itself with the critics of religion, and conquered the ancient and early European heathen world, so that Christianity begot the digger of its own grave? Or are the questions which Christianity, in the days of late antiquity, allied itself with itself, since it also is only a phase of the early onset of forgetfulness of being, which, as Heidegger believes, begins as early as the transition from the pre-Socratic thinkers to Plato, so that Nietzsche called Christianity a "Platonism for the people".[6] How far back, and how deep does the questioning go in which Christianity is involved in its encounter with Marxism? Is it only superficially grazed by the questions of Communism, can these be easily parried, perhaps even justly returned on Communism's own head, or are we driven by them to undertake a theological revision as radical as was the transformation of the outward form of the church's life to which it was indubitably subjected in the transition from the "capitalistic" to the "socialistic" society? This revision would not be a sign of the fact that, as a result of the dispute with Marxism, the Christian faith had become uncertain of itself, but it would be a sign of the fact that this dispute had called in question the Church's historical forms of expression, its forms of thought, and its forms of life, which it must in any case repeatedly submit to question, and with which it must never identify itself and the gospel to which it owes its existence, if it is to continue to be free and obedient Christian faith.

[6] Preface to *Jenseits von Gut und Böse*, 1885.

(b) How is the Christian faith to encounter Marxism? The latter belongs from the beginning not only to the history of ideas, but as a programme for changing the world it belongs to the history of society. But this is equally true of Christianity, which always at once has results that are formative of reality. How is the mission of the Christian faith to a world shaped by Marxism to be rightly understood and carried through? What in this world is encountered by the "No" of the Christian faith? Where and how far can one collaborate? Where and how far can co-operation take place? What does it mean for the Church when it must confess that in the power of Communism not merely human hostility encounters it, but a deeper question? Is it the abyss of Antichrist and Satan—or is it the abyss of the Providence of God —or both at once? The analysis of Marxist atheism is unavoidable, but it has this danger, that it fixes Marxism as a static entity, inescapably and hopelessly unalterable, that it reduces it to principles whose dictates govern not it alone, but equally the behaviour of the Christian who encounters it in pure reaction. It must be evident how little in the Bible the enemies of God's people are analysed. Their doctrines are not given the honour of an independent interest, their principles and their self-understanding are not there taken nearly so seriously as we today believe we must do even in this Commission of ours; they are passed over, and all seriousness is concentrated on the question: "What does God intend in relation to God's people by permitting the existence of such enemies?" The Philistines, Nebuchadnezzar, Pilate, and the persecutors of the primitive Church are regarded as servants and tools of God, whose government is not limited by their power, but confirms itself by means of them, and God uses their chastening to chasten his people.[7]

That God's people must not capitulate in face of the enmity, the slanders, and the attacks upon its message and its

[7] Cf. J. Hamel, *Christenheit unter marxistischer Herrschaft*, Berlin, 1959, pp. 7f.

existence, is clear from the start. But not every "No" is a "No" obedient to God simply because it is a "No". The resistance of Jerusalem to Nebuchadnezzar's men and Peter's sword-stroke against Malchus (John 18:10f.) are not acknowledged as the true "No" of faith. What belongs to the right answer of God's people, in which there must inevitably be contained a "No"—this question is raised so soon as we see that a reaction which simply pays back in the same or a similar coin, is one which is certainly forbidden by our Christian faith. If our faith challenges us to see that behind the oppressing powers the Lord of the Church is himself effectively at work, then his people understands that it has been sent into a continually changing world in which ever new phenomena of hostility and friendship, of idolatry and Enlightenment must serve the best interests, that is, the best interests of its service. For this service then admittedly in our situation of today an analysis of the opposing doctrine is unavoidable. We must be ready to criticize ourselves, to weigh carefully the arguments and questions brought forward, and hold an open conversation with our opponents. And so the kind of work which is being done in our Commission is necessary, if only we take good care that it does not harden our first sense of antagonism, but rather brings it into new movement.

CHAPTER TWO

The Criticism of Religion in Karl Marx and Friedrich Engels

The Marxist "No" to Religion

THE following points are to be noted in the Marxist repudiation of religion:

1. The repudiation stems from Marxism, i.e. its initiative lies with the so-called classical Marxists; it did not merely develop at a later stage as a reaction to certain experiences.

2. It is from the first decisive and uncompromising.

3. In this it exhibits an essential criterion which distinguishes Marxism from early socialism.

4. The denial of religion is not a central theme of Marxism, but rather the result of a development already complete in principle.

5. This denial is made in a world which for centuries had been in some measure influenced by Christian preaching, and must therefore have some connection with this fact.

6. It makes no distinction, either positive or negative, between Christianity and the other religions, and does not admit the possibility that there might be better forms of Christianity which would not be subject to the general condemnation.[1]

7. This repudiation is openly avowed and claimed to be an essential element in the struggle for the society of the future and an anticipation of the final spiritual condition of this

[1] This all holds as a matter of principle, and thus does not mean that in practice the Marxist is not perfectly able to distinguish between more positive and more negative representations of the Christian faith.

society of the future. It is also averred to be obligatory on the party in spite of all temptations to disguise it or keep it secret for the sake of political opportunism.

In contrast with the other political movements of modern times, with their manifold phases and tendencies, this attitude so cut-and-dried and intransigent, this attitude at once marked by rigidity and finality in the face of a problem of human life so indeterminate and never finally comprehended as that of religion, is an astonishing phenomenon. It betrays a dogmatic claim which arouses the suspicion of doctrinaire narrowness, and therefore initially tends to prejudice one against the person who makes it. This causes us to inquire into the origin of the phenomenon and must not hinder us from taking it seriously. We are thus led to inquire about the place of the teaching concerning religion within Marxist theory, concerning its motives and the degree of necessity which binds it to the whole structure of the theory.

We choose for presentation one of the most familiar texts of Marx, the excellently formulated introduction "A Criticism of Hegel's Philosophy of Right", whose theses have themselves acquired historical significance, because they have made a profound impression on men's minds.[2] It begins with the sentence *"For Germany, the criticism of religion is essentially completed, and the criticism of religion is the presupposition of all criticism."*

[2] I quote from S. Landshut's *Karl Marx, Frühschriften,* Stuttgart, 1953 (later cited as *Frühschriften*), pp. 207f. It is significant that Marx's utterances on the question of religion are to be found almost exclusively in the writings of his early period (Works in Preparation for the Dissertation, Paris manuscripts, Introduction to his "Critique of the Hegelian Philosophy of Right", "The Holy Family", "The German Ideology"). Engels, on the contrary, like Lenin, concerned himself all his life long with the problem of religion. In his case special reference must be made to the *Anti-Dühring* the "Dialectic of Nature" and his writing on Feuerbach. The most important texts are conveniently gathered together in K. Marx and F. Engels *Ueber die Religion,* East Berlin, 1958. Cf. A. Rich, "Die kryptoreligiösen Motive in den Frühschriften von K. Marx", in *Theologische Zeitschriften,* Basle, 1951 (later cited as Th. Z.).

What the context of this criticism of religion is, we have yet to describe. Marx asserts only its completion; its task is done, its object has been seen through, and now only the consequences of this are of interest, i.e. the possibilities which open up as a result. Of these Marx speaks in the next two sentences. "Its *profane* existence is refuted, since its *heavenly Oratio pro aris et focis* is refuted. The man who has found only the *reflection* of himself in the imaginary reality where he sought a superman, will no more be inclined to find only the *appearance* of himself, only an unreal man, where he seeks and must seek his true reality."

If man's search in the heavenly places is ended, because instead of the superman he longed for, only his own reflection is to be found there (as the preceding criticism of religion has established), then man *must* seek his true reality here below, and since now, because of the acknowledged emptiness of heaven, he can no more return to the search above, he will be "no more inclined" to content himself with his failure to find anything more than inhumanity in the sphere of his "true reality". This appears to be the heart of the matter for Marx, his interest that the way upwards should be blocked by the proof that it is a cul-de-sac, is based on his central interest that man should no longer be deflected by anything from the sphere of his earthly life as the sphere of his "true reality", that he should no longer in any manner be lifted up by any consolation above the misery of this sphere, so that this misery should become intolerable to him, and that, without relying any more on help from other sources, he should set himself the task of altering this reality of his (11th Thesis on Feuerbach!), i.e. that he should transform it from an inhuman reality into a human one. "Our criticism has plucked the imaginary flowers from the chain, not in order that man should wear the forlorn chain stripped of its phantasies, but in order that he should throw the chain away, and pick living flowers", says Marx, a few sentences later. It is just its consolatory character, which the defenders of religion urge in its favour, which causes Marx to reject religion as a temptation, as a paralysing opiate. Consolation is reprehensible, when one consoles oneself about a condition which one could alter through revolt and struggle. Religion is "the opium of the people", i.e. the consolation which the people provides for itself because it does not dare to revolt, or does not know the way to victory. The man who takes away from it this consolation does the same good service as one who takes away the opium pipe from the coolie. "The struggle against religion is thus at one remove the struggle against that world whose spiritual aroma is religion." Thus the denial of religion is not an end in itself, but a fighting doctrine; its source is not a theoretical interest for truth, but the practical interest in the changing of this world into a human one. Here speaks an "unreligious" man in Bonhoeffer's sense of the concept. He is led, neither by religious nor by anti-religious emotion, but only by interest in this world and the removal of its misery. Thus we must at once note that what is here called "the struggle against religion" is entirely dependent on whether and how far what is here ascribed to religion is applicable. And with this the question is put to the representatives of religion, the Christians, whether they can deny that it is applicable, and in what way, if the central verdict should be reversible, the false impression arose. Was it elicited by an inadequate representation of religion? Can it be annulled? Its annulment would alter the whole situation.

Marx himself allows no possibility of this. He speaks in general terms of "religion", makes no exception in the case of any existing religion, and brings them all boldly under the one common denominator. It must not be overlooked that this would not have been possible either in the time of the apostles or in that of the Middle Ages and the Reformation, but depends on a typical presupposition of modern times. Since the Enlightenment the antithesis between Christianity and the religions has been regarded merely as an antithesis on a common basis, and Christianity has been defended against its critics in the following manner. First of all religion in general has been defended as a fundamental human possibility, as a legitimate need of man to reverence that which is above him, that which is the ground both of his being and of the rest of the world. And then Christianity has been proved to be the highest development of this possibility.[3] Thus a special presupposition of the preceding theology, a special *theological* view of the relation of the Christian message to the religions is the presupposition upon which Marx without further inquiry bases himself. A critical discussion of his view will have to take into consideration also the theology which he presupposes.

Excursus on the expression "Opium of the People"

The origin of the opium simile was first investigated by Reinhart Seeger.[4] He found Bruno Bauer as "the creator of the word", Moses Hess and Karl Marx as the "imitators and popularizers", and indeed the reference to Bauer is to his essay *Der Christliche Staat and unsere Zeit*,[4a] in which Bauer says that the "theological organisation in the most Christian State was able to 'carry matters so far through its opium-like influence' that it finds no more trace of resistance and all the instincts of free humanity . . . are lulled to sleep". In the next year he writes that religion speaks, after it has trodden everything underfoot, "in the opium haze of its destructive malady" of a new condition hereafter. His brother Edgar takes this up in one of his short stories, with the sentence, "Others drug themselves with religion, they would wish to enter the seventh

[3] Cf. the survey dealing with the development of the concept of religion in K. Barth, *Church Dogmatics,* Edinburgh, 1956 (I, 2 pp. 284f.).

[4] R. Seeger, "Herkunft und Bedeutung des Schlagwortes: Die Religion ist Opium für das Volk" in *Theologische Arbeiten zur Bibel-Kirchen- und Geistesgeschichte,* ed. E. Barnikol, Halle, 1935, III p. 45).

[4a] *Hallisches Jahrbuch.* Halle, 1841, IV, 537f.

heaven, and in so doing forget the earth."[4b] As a next stage, Moses Hess comes even closer to the Marxist formula, in his *Einundzwanzig Bogen aus der Schweiz*,[4c] of which Marx thought highly. Hess ranks side by side the "intoxicants, opium, religion, and brandy" and says "Religion is well able . . . to make tolerable the unhappy consciousness of servitude . . . just as opium does good service in painful illnesses, faith in the reality of unreality and in the unreality of reality can indeed give the sufferer a passive happiness . . . but it cannot give the manly energy to free oneself from the evil."[4d]

Seeger refers to the Opium War of Britain against China, 1839–1842, which may have given special point to this comparison, and he also cites as a preliminary influence— Goethe's criticism of the volume of sermons, *Blick ins Reich der Gnade* (1828) of F. W. Krummacher, the well-known revivalistic preacher.[5] Goethe speaks of the life of the factory operatives and workers in the Barmen district and is of the opinion that these men, in the prose of their lives, are well disposed for this type of "narcotic sermons". Whether these lines of Goethe were known to the young Friedrich Engels is uncertain; at any rate there is in his "Letters from Wuppertal" not only a vivid and satirical description of Krummacher's manner of preaching,[6] which bears out Goethe's judgment but also uses a similar comparison: "Such of these people who do not fall into the hands of mysticism, succumb to brandy". "There sits the master, on

[4b] *Die Gute Sache der Freiheit und meine eigene Angelegenheit*, Zürich and Winterthur, 1842, 212.

[4c] Ed. G. Herwegh. Zürich and Winterthur. 1843.

[4d] Page 95.

[5] J. W. von Goethe, 1857, vol. 32, p. 379. Cf. Uckeley in *Die Religion in Geschichte und Gegenwart* (later referred to as RGG) 2nd ed., III, 1329. The unfair picture which Seeger gives of pietism on this occasion, is rightly corrected by K. Kupisch, *Von Pietismus zum Kommunismus*, Berlin, 1953, 41.

[6] *Marx-Engels: Gesammelte Aufsatze* (lated cited as MEGA) I, 2, p. 30.

his right hand the Bible, on his left, at least very often, the brandy."[7] In a similar sense writes another author from the circle of "Young Germany" about the much-talked-of Wuppertal pietists: "They must intoxicate themselves, bodily and spiritually, in order to revive their exhausted nerves. . . . The revelations of religion are here the only balm for the repressed anxieties of life."[8]

Seeger has shown that the comparison of religion with intoxicants was in the air. His demonstration can, however, be made more complete, and the historical line can be traced further into the past. In the first place, as Ewald Schaper has shown,[9] Seeger's assertion that there are no parallel passages in Feuerbach,[9a] is not true. In the notes and explanations of the first edition of his *Pierre Bayle*, Feuerbach writes: "The man therefore who charms with enticing and flattering words of eternal joys and threatens separation from himself with the intimidating words of eternal hell, used methods of compulsion, and employs an unspiritual, immoral, and base means of winning a man for himself; he administers opium to him to extract from him his word of honour in a condition where the passions of fear or hope have clouded his vision."[9b] Without the figure of opium he expresses himself similarly in *The Nature of Christianity*,[9c] and speaks there of the "narcotic influences" of the spoken word,[9d] and also of the "halo of sanctity" with which Christianity surrounds marriage in order to cloud the reason.[9e] Schaper is further of the opinion that not only the Opium War, but even before it, the case of the foundling Kaspar Hauser, who played a large part in Feuerbach's father's house, with the discussions started by him about the influences of drugs, may have suggested such comparisons to him.

[7] Ibid. 25.
[8] G. Kühne, *Männliche und weibliche Charaktere*, 1938, pp. 270ff.
[9] "Religion ist Opium fürs Volk" in *Zeitschrift für Kirchengeschichte,* 1940, pp. 425–29.
[9a] Seeger, op. cit. 34.   [9b] 1838, p. 249.   [9c] 1st ed. 1841, p. 250.
[9d] Ibid. p. 94.   [9e] Ibid. p. 420.

In the circle of Marx, in addition to Proudhon,[10] mention must be made of Heinrich Heine. The latter wrote in 1840 in the fourth book of his discussion with Ludwig Börne: "As the individual opens his arteries in despair, and seeks in death a refuge from the tyranny of the Caesars, so the great mass plunged into asceticism, into the doctrines of mortification . . . into the whole suicide of the Nazarene religion, in order once and for all to thrust from itself the misery of life at that time . . . in order to number their aching heads with organ-tones and the tolling of bells". "For men for whom earth has nothing more to offer, heaven is invented. . . . Hail to this invention! Hail to a religion which poured for a suffering race of men some sweet narcotic drops into their bitter cup, spiritual opium, a few drops of love and hope and faith."[11] Ten years later, in a very different situation and frame of mind, he said on his "mattress-tomb" to Adolf Stahr and Fanny Lewald "I have also my religion. Do not think that I am without religion. Opium is also a religion. . . . When a little grey dust is poured into my fearful burning wounds, and then the pain at once ceases, shall one not say that this is the same calming power which shows its effectiveness in religion? There is more relationship between opium and religion than most men dream."[12]

Of especial influence may have been the fact that Hegel in his *Religionsphilosophie*,[13] compared Indian religion to a man "decayed in body and spirit, who finds his existence grown

---

[10] In the memoir of his youth, Proudhon tells us that his uncle had often said that religion was as necessary for man as bread, and as dangerous as poison; where his uncle got this saying, he does not know, but he has later learnt to value it (quoted in M. Reding, *Der politische Atheismus*, 1957, 125).

[11] *Sämtliche Werke*, vol. 8, p. 478. Cf. on this point P. Meinhold, "Zur Religionskritik von H. Heine und K. Marx" in *Monatsschrift für Pastoraltheologie, Göttingen*, 1969, pp. 161–76; also E. Kux, "Marx und Heine" in *Neue Zürcher Zeitung* of 11.2.1956, p. 4.

[12] H. H. Houben, *Gespräche mit Heinrich Heine*, 2nd ed., Potsdam. 1948, pp. 770f.

[13] *Reclam-Ausgabe* of F. Brunstäd, p. 229.

dull and insufferable" and is therefore at pains to create for himself with opium "a dreaming world and crazy happiness". Ernst Benz[14] has illuminatingly shown how the young Hegelians, eagerly and without hesitation, ascribed to Christianity, the same negative phenomena which Hegel had indicated in this passage in Indian, Greek, and Roman religion. They did the same with Hegel's judgment that in Indian religion we find a dehumanizing of man, and a "contempt for life".

Further back we find a similar thought in a letter from Gass to Schleiermacher in the year 1822. "It becomes ever clearer how close an alliance there is between modern piety and the narrow-minded aristocracy, and how the former is used by the latter in order to deflect men's intellectual and moral powers from their right object."[15] Thus many phenomena of the romantic movement of revival, with their excited emotionalism and their individualistic interest in salvation may have given occasion to such comparison, with its critical tendency.

I find the earliest passage in the modern criticism of religion, which tasks religion with a narcotic effect, which is in the interest of the governing class, in a quotation from P. T. von Holbach, *Le Christianisme dévoile*,[15a] which is cited

[14] *Heges Religionsphilosophie und die Linkshegelianer. Zur Kritik des Religionsbegriffes von Karl Marx, Zeitschrift für Religions- und Geistesgeschichte*, 7th Year, 1955, pp. 247-70.
The expression "dream-world" for religion, which is only "passivity and emptiness of the spirit" recurs in B. Bauer, *Des Entdeckte Christentum im Vormärz* (1943), ed. E. Barnikol, Jena, 1927, p. 3. It may be mentioned that the comparison is also to be found in Kant, who, in his "Religion within the Bounds of Reason Alone" speaks "of the forgiveness of sins as 'opium for the conscience'". (Kant's Works, published by Weischedel, 3rd Volume, p. 733 Note.)

[15] *Schleiermachers Briefwechsel mit Gass*, Berlin, 1852, p. 192; cf. p. 140. In similar vein Schleiermacher himself wrote earlier in the second edition of his *Reden* (1806), p. 171: "The piety of the Revival betrays by its indifference to all great world affairs and by its impatient lovelessness a deeply rooted malady".

[15a] 1761. p. 226.

by Schmidt. "Religion is the art of making men *drunk* with enthusiasm, in order to hinder them from attending to the evils with which those who rule them overwhelm them here below. With the help of the invisible powers with which one threatens them, one compels them to bear the misery in silence with which the powerful afflict them, one makes them hope that, if they consent to be unhappy in this world, they will be more happy in another."[16]

The criticism contained in 'this comparison, which is to be taken seriously, and can without difficulty be supported by examples from the past and from the present, loses its justice when it does not distinguish. The generalization, which the circle of Marx eagerly accepted, is also its weakness. If once Leonhard Ragaz said that the New Testament message of the Kingdom of God was "not opium, but dynamite", an open-minded Marxism, such as is represented by Ernst Bloch, finds itself forced to draw a distinction between the non-narcotic function of religion in "the great religious teachers", and its narcotic function in priestlings.[17] And there is a further distinction to which that melancholy word of suffering of the later Heine points, there is a positive resignation (not to be confused with a lifeless or other-worldly submission), which not only accepts the inevitable, but inwardly appropriates it and thus draws from it active powers to overcome and resist, so that the vision itself of a transcendent hope sets us free for a new vision of hope for this world. The young Hegelians and Marxists were never able, in their interest in the primitive antithesis "Resistance *or* resignation", to value the conjunction "Resistance *and* resignation" (Bonhoeffer), which has such an incalculable significance for human life, and in which the authentic nature of faith expresses itself. And so they were also blind to the alleviation and humanization which—in sharp distinction

[16] Article *Deismus in* RGG, 3rd Edition, vol 2, especially p. 67.

[17] *Das Prinzip Hoffnung,* vol. 3, p. 385, references to the catchword are to be found on pp. 200, 299, 334, 337, 343, 370.

from the dull passivity of apathy and despair—is introduced by this attitude of faith into the struggle for life on earth. With an eye upon this the prominent Sinhalese Christian, Daniel T. Niles, can even venture to evaluate the opium catch-word positively. "The gospel gives the struggle for life its meaning and at the same time demotes it to the second place. . . . Bread is given significance of serving as a help to true life and the struggle for bread is freed from the bitterness it can cause. It is true that religion is opium for the masses; for genuine religion alleviates the desire for revenge."[18]

But to close with a phrase of self-criticism; there is an over-hasty misuse of the answer, which the Christian message implies for human problems. This occurs when the message is applied as if it were a pat and ready answer, lying ready to our hand, an answer which stifles inquiry. The message is in reality not in our possession, it is rather the promise of an answer, which actually makes the man who hears it in faith capable of bearing the burden of questions without answering them. That is what Reinhold Schneider means in one of his late memoranda, which also uses the comparison dealt with here. "Or do we perhaps believe that there are aspects of the world to which Christianity has no answer? That is the only thing that must not happen. And it is better to die with a burning question on one's heart than with a not quite honest faith."[18a]

Another picture that is important for Marx is taken from the field of comparative religion, and serves him in his hostile characterization of religious life in general, and is then

---

[18] *Die Botschaft für die Welt,* Munich, 1960, p. 38f. That this can one day be of interest even for a Communist system, is indicated by Princess Schakowskoy's report on Russia, *So sah ich Russland wieder;* she speaks of the embitterment among the people, which could one day become dangerous for their leaders, so that the latter have actually less to fear from the Christians oppressed by them than from the unchurched masses.

[18a] R. Schneider, *Pfeiler im Strom,* 1958, p. 242.

carried over into the field of economics. It is the figure of the *fetish*. I have been unable to discover whether there has been a similar long tradition in this case. Perhaps Marx himself came upon the comparison through his studies in comparative religion (1842), which also touched on fetishism.[19] At any rate at that early date he says in his essay on the Rhenish Law about wood-stealing, that as once the savages in Cuba had held that gold was the fetish of the Spaniards, they would now hold that wood was the fetish of the Rhinelanders. In the Paris manuscripts (1844) he calls the mercantilists "fetish worshippers" because they see the essence of private property in the object, and not in the labour.[20] At the same time he writes, without indeed using himself the figure, in the essay "On the Jewish Question": "Money is the jealous god of Israel, before whom no other god can stand. Money brings low all the gods of men—and transforms them into a commodity", and similarly again in the Paris manuscripts, "money is the visible deity . . . the divine power of money lies in its nature. It is the alienated wealth of humanity."[21] After 1848 he may have read Feuerbach's twentieth lecture on the nature of religion, in which it was shown, by taking the example of fetishism, how man can make every material thing, natural things as well as his own productions, into a divine being strange to himself. And this nonsense has a very real significance; by falsely ascribing human emotions to a thing, man betrays that he has an inkling of the truth that only man can help man. And so we come in conclusion to the magnificent chapter on the "fetishism of commodities" in the first volume of *Das Kapital* in which the mercantile form of the product of labour is described as the "phantasmagoric form of a relationship of things, which is the concealed form of a particular social relationship between

[19] Cf. his "Excerpts" MEGA I, 1/2; from these is taken his observation in the essay against the *Kölnische Zeitung*, 1842, "On Religion", p. 15.

[20] *Frühschriften*, p. 228 and p. 264.

[21] Ibid. p. 204 and p. 299.

men: Thus to find an anology, we must fly up to the cloudy region of the religious world. Here the products of the human mind appear endowed with their own life, independent forms standing in relation to each other and to men. So it is in the world of commodities with the products of the human hand. This I call fetishism, which adheres to the products of labour, so soon as they are produced as commodities."[22]

The Non-Religious Type

Such an inquiry,[22a] concerning the theory of religion, has long been proceeding in contemporary Protestant theology. Apart from the fact that in this area different central problems of Christian theology are involved, there is a preliminary difficulty about terminology, since it is hardly possible to get a sufficient agreement as to what is meant by "religion", how far the concept is limited by reference to the historic religions and to fixed forms of a belief in God, or whether it includes also the phenomenon of unattached religiosity, which as a mood and tendency can be associated not less with an atheistic ideology than with supernatural doctrines. The antithesis between atheism and religion is, as a phenomenon of religion, certainly only superficial. E. Sarkisyanz[23] has vividly shown how local religious impulses and expectations streamed into the Communist movement as soon as it found a foothold in the East. Paul Tillich's concept of the religious has its validity independently of definite ideas and doctrines, and in his earlier period Tillich wished to demonstrate that even proletarian Socialism was an upsurge of religious forces. Clearly a very much more restricted phenomenon was indicated by Dietrich Bonhoeffer when he conjectured that

[22] *Das Kapital*, vol. I, pp. 77f.—cf. on this point the analysis of the "concept of Fetishism"; Ruth-Eva Schulz, "Geschichte und teleologisches System bei K. Marx", *Plessner-Festschrift*, 1958, pp. 164ff.
[22a] Cf. p. 18, *supra*.
[23] *Russland und der Messianismus des Orients*, Tübingen, 1955.

"the time of inwardness and conscience—and that means the time of religion in general", was finished today, and that we were entering "a completely religionless time".[24] If Bonhoeffer denied the intention of himself becoming a *homo religiosus*[24a] he must have been thinking of a type of "inwardness" which he believed had first been discovered in the Renaissance,[24b] and which he regarded as "something partial" in contrast to faith as a total act of life.[24c] Thus for him religiosity was understood as a typological concept; it describes a particular type of man, who has had his day, and with whom another type—the profane man—can be set in contrast. Without going into detailed discussion about Bonhoeffer's critical attitude to "religion" in this sense, and apart from the question of the correctness of his judgment about the times, it will have to be conceded that we can speak of religion also in this sense, which involves distinguishing between individual and cultural types. This difficulty of determining a common concept, which makes every assertion about religion like stumbling in a pathless wilderness, must be kept in mind in all our subsequent discussion. At this point it is only mentioned in order to characterize the Marxist talk about religion. Nowhere do Marx and Engels betray a consciousness of the difficulty we have described. "Criticism of religion" is for them taken for granted as criticism with a negative result, "irreligious criticism" as Marx says in our text. "Religion, philosophy . . . have a prehistoric status, inherited and taken over by the historical period, a status of what we would today call nonsense",[25] they confront with condescending contempt this omnium-gatherum of different false conceptions of nature, of the character of man himself, of spirits, magic powers, etc.,[25a]

[24] *Letters and Papers from Prison*, London, 1967 (Revised).
[24a] Ibid. p. 97.
[24b] Ibid. p. 192.
[24c] Ibid. p.   .
[25] F. Engels to Conrad Scheidt, 27.10.1890, in *Ueber die Religion*— cf. Note 8, p. 228.
[25a] Ibid.

while in Lenin there is a continual unmistakable note of hatred—while further the manner in which Lenin is everywhere on the lookout to trace and stop the slightest holes where "fideism" might leak in, betrays that he is more sensitive than his spiritual fathers to the breadth and the manifold forms of religion, though admittedly even he does not seek a place for it on any other intellectual plane than on that of pernicious ideas.[26]

None of them agreed with Schleiermacher's anti-rationalistic expansion and de-intellectualization of the concept of religion.[27] It may be conjectured that Feuerbach's influence was already at work with a paralysing effect; Schleiermacher's religion of feeling, discredited in any case by Hegel's criticism in the eyes of the younger men, appeared to them as an apologetic device to rescue religion from the inexorable rational question as to its truth-content.

But this also betrays that the emotions to which Schleiermacher and his followers appealed, awoke no echo of sympathy in them. In the sense of the typological concept of "religious" as opposed to "profane", as Bonhoeffer used it, and a man like Mircea Eliade has illustrated with rich material,[28] they declare themselves convinced advocates of the profane. With these young men a kind of socialism which has done with religion, and all that "smells" of religion, enters the world, and for which, as socialism, it is essential to have done

[26] Cf. especially Lenin's letters to Gorki of November and December 1913, against the "Hunger for God" of Gorki, Lunatscharski, etc. (in W. J. Lenin *Ueber die Religion,* East Berlin, 1956, pp. 44f.).

[27] The brief encounter of the young Engels with Schleiermacher made him indeed write to his friend, F. Gaber: "Religion is a thing of the heart, and the man who has a heart can be religious . . . that is Schleiermacher's teaching, and I stand by it", but this cannot alter the fact that this encounter came too late for him: "Had I known the teaching earlier, I would never have become a rationalist, but where does one hear anything of this kind in our canting world?" MEGA I, 2, pp. 531, 527.

[28] M. Eliade, *Das Heilige und das Profane. Vom Wesen des Religiösen,* Hamburg, 1957, especially the concluding section on "Heliges und Profanes in der modernen welt" (pp. 119ff.).

with religion. If early socialism had distinguished itself from the Christian tradition by its decisive claim to the right to happiness in this world, so now, in opposition to religion, there was added the claim to rationality and absolute independence. "The modern irreligious man . . . accepts no kind of humanity except the human disposition as it can be recognized in the different historical situations. Man makes himself, and he can only really make himself in the measure that he desacralizes himself and the world."[29] The individual constitution of the Marxist classical writers and the "totally desacralized world" of the modern era[30] correspond one to the other. The "profane" type must have existed at all times, but it has not been at all times equally able to express itself—not only because of the existent prohibitions, but because it had no means of expression, and therefore was hardly conscious of its own character. Because it was only able to express its lack of sympathy with religious emotions by means of a merely conventional participation in the religious life of its environment, it was possible for the impression to arise that religious feelings were universal, and that every man could be claimed to have them. But the negative thesis that there are completely irreligious men, and the positive one, that in every man, though often buried, or hardly developed, the need for religion is slumbering—both these belong to the realm of assertions which can never be fully proved. It can only be said that modern times bring the irreligious type

[29] Ibid. p. 120.
[30] Ibid. p. 9. "The word, desacralized in its totality, the wholly desacralized Cosmos, is a new discovery in the history of the human spirit. . . . It is enough for us to observe that desacralization is the hallmark of the total experience of the non-religious man of modern societies, and that in consequence it is becoming ever more difficult for this man to rediscover the existential dimensions of the archaic societies." On the modern "Desacralization" as a theological problem cf. H. Thielicke, "Das Ende der Religion" in *Theologische Literaturzeitung* and Wilhelm Hahn "Säkularisation und Religionszerfall" in *Kerygma und Dogma*, 1959, pp. 83-98. C. H. Ratschow, Article in RGG, 3rd Ed. V, 1288ff.

into the foreground, and give him a language, so that he becomes its representative type, with his rationality and his concentration on this world and the shaping of it. Marx himself, with his lack of interest in religion in every form, even in the struggle against religion, is a prominent representative of this type. For the Christian Church this phenomenon implies the question whether it regards itself as a particular case of religion. If so, then as far as this type is concerned, it allocates itself a place among things in principle dead and gone. Or if it presupposes a universal religious sensitivity to its message, then its effectiveness will depend on its success in awakening this possibility of contact even in men of the irreligious type (otherwise it must resign itself to failure in their case). Another possibility would be that it has a quite different word to bring than the religions, a word which has its own power, which does not depend on aerials already present, but is able to make its own impact; and that in consequence, it is able to express what it has to say without borrowing from the world of religious traditions. If the latter is the case—and the way in which a Jahweh, the "living God" of Israel in the Old Testament, stands against the gods, and in which the cross of Jesus in the New Testament is the common work of men of the religious and the profane type, suggests that this is the case—then the difference between the two types will have to be relativized for the Church, through confidence in that power of its message to which it refers when it speaks of the Holy Spirit. Then the transition from a religious age to an irreligious one will not be a catastrophe for it, but will only signify a new task.

The Character of Anti-Religious Criticism

Marx took it just as much for granted as did the theology of his time, that Christian faith was a phenomenon within the world of religions, and nothing more. In the whole of modern times we have to distinguish between three kinds of criticism[31] concerning the life of religion. There is a criticism of the empirical Church, which is compatible with a convinced affirmation of the Christian faith; its line of tradition runs from the medieval movements, which were critical of the Church (spiritual men of the Franciscan type, Waldensians, etc.), down to the socialism of our days. There is a criticism of Christianity as a religion in some ways harmful, or specially defective, without all religion being condemned at the same time. Such criticism is to be found, for example, in Machiavelli—Christianity weakens the manly virtues,[31a] in Rousseau —Christianity makes men incapable of political action.[31b] This criticism increases with the possibility of comparing religions through the knowledge of the great Asiatic religions. Finally, there is the criticism of *religion* as such, which only ventured to raise its head here and there before the Enlightenment, and for the first time raised its voice loud and clear in the French Enlightenment. Marxism takes over from Feuerbach, the latter kind of criticism; early socialism limits itself to the first.

This difference between the socialist theoreticians is striking, and has important consequences; it compels us to ask the question (which will concern us later) as to the real motives of the Marxist decision. Of the notable early socialists hardly one could be said to have had a living relationship to Christian piety. To all of them its outlook on a transcendent life is alien. They are irritated by the irrationality of earthly conditions, interested in science, concentrated on the problem of earthly happiness and the increase of the possibilities of earthly happiness for all, all of them are repelled by the fatalism with which, under the influence of religion, the people accept the pressure

[31] Here I adopt a distinction which Professor Eric Weil, Lille, used in his address on "The Modern Secularization of Politics and Political Thinking" at the Session of the Commission on Marxism in October 1958. To this lecture I owe also the reference to Machiavelli.

[31a] *Discorsi* II, 2; III, 1.

[31b] *Contrat Social* IV, 8.

of their circumstances. They are uninterested in religious questions in the narrower sense, but their criticism is directed only against the Church, as it unfortuntely is. From the beginning Jesus is looked on as the antithesis of official Christianity, and is regarded, long before Kautsky, as the first socialist. "The repudiation of power and riches, self-abasement and self-sacrifice were the basis of the teaching of Christ"—as we read in Weitling's *Die Menschheit, wie sie ist, und wie sie sein sollte*. It was through Constantine that this was changed: "Since that time a dark night has brooded over the pure principles of Christianity. The kingdom of deceit and violence began. Millions perished in their poisonous talons, and under protection of darkness, the monsters continued their destructive work in the hearts of the peoples."[32] Correspondingly the writer's own struggle is understood and represented as the renewal of original Christianity, or as the modernization and further development of contemporary Christianity, which is still too much a prisoner of the past. Henri de Saint-Simon calls one of his chief works *Le nouveau Christianisme* (1825) and in it urges the transcendence of the opposition between faith and science through the modernization of Church doctrine and the love of our neighbour as the basic principle of the organization of society. "Religion has the task of leading society to the great goal of as speedy an improvement as possible of the situation of the poorest class."[33] Shortly after, Charles Fourier tried in his book *Le Nouveau Monde* (1829) to support his theory by the gospels; his *doctrine sociétaire* was, he claimed, *l'expression du vrai Christianisme de Jésus*: he conceives of the social problem as a religious one, as the return of man to God.[34] The followers of Saint-Simon develop the system of their master further as a religious theory,[35] down

[32] Quoted from T. Ramm, *Die grossen Sozialisten als Rechts- und Staatsphilosophen*, vol I, 1955, p. 510.

[33] Quoted from T. Ramm, Ibid. p. 325.

[34] So T. Ramm, Ibid. p. 325.

[35] Cf. the account in T. Ramm, Ibid. p. 288–313, and the text printed in Ramm, *Der Frühsozialismus*, Stuttgart, 1956, p. 68.

to the Catholic Socialism of P. J. B. Buchez. Wilhelm Weitling wrote in 1843 *Das Evangelium eines armen Sünders* as an exposition of words of the gospels[36] and wrote for the children of members of his "Labour Union" the following touching and comical hymn:

> I am a little Communist,
>   And riches I disdain,
> Because our Master Jesus Christ
>   Sought neither gold nor gain.
>
> I am a little Communist,
>   And shall be kind and true,
> And later as a Christian join
>   The Labour Union, too.[37]

The rupture between him and Marx came about in Brussels in 1846, precisely because Marx condemned all this sentimentalism about a socialism of love, which had become fashionable through Feuerbach, as concealed Christianity.

It is clear how questionable everything is which these dreamers write about Christianity, how questionable also are the motives for their attempts to link up with Christianity; calculation as well as romantic fashion play their part. But this meant that the door was still open—and if the opportunity had been used, then, as the English example shows—the relations between the Labour movement and Christian circles might have developed very differently. But now Marxism on its side slammed the door, too. Why it did so, we shall later have to ask. At first we must only state what it has to say of religion. What, in its opinion, is the nature of religion?

Answer: It has "as religion, neither a nature nor a place".

[36] Cf. the excerpt in *Der Frühsozialismus*, pp. 322–60.
[37] According to T. Ramm, *Die grossen Sozialisten*, vol. I, p. 512, 95n.

For "In religion men make their empirical world a mere thought-world, a world of ideas, which confronts them as a strange reality. This in its turn is by no means to be explained through other concepts, as a product of '*man's* self-consciousness', or other twaddle of the same kind, but as the product of the whole preceding means of production and trade, which is just as independent of a concept as the invention of the self-acting mule and the use of the railways is independent of the Hegelian philosophy. If he (Stirner) wishes to speak of a 'nature of religion'—i.e. of a material foundation of this absurdity, then he must seek it neither in the 'nature of man' nor in the predicates of God, but in the material world which is presupposed in every stage of religious development.[38] Nor is there any change in the view of the later Engels: "Now all religion is nothing but the fantastic reflection in men's heads of those external powers which dominate their daily life, a reflection in which earthly powers take on the form of supernatural ones."[39]

The teaching about the nature of religion is thus at once a judgment about its relation to reality; the powers of which religion speaks are in reality quite other powers. In the form of which religion speaks of them they exist only in the imagination of man, they are human ideas. But ideas in relation to the man who thinks them, are not primary, but secondary. "Men are the producers of their conceptions, ideas, etc., but real, producing actual men, as they are conditioned by a definite development of their productive powers and the intercourse which corresponds with these, up to its most far-reaching formations."[40] In the schema of the medieval debate about universals, here the position of nominalism is at once adopted.

[38] K. Marx/F. Engels, *Die deutsche Ideologie*, new edition of the Dietz-Verlag, East Berlin, 1953, p. 159.

[39] *Herrn Eugen Dührings Umwälzung der Wissenschaft* (Anti-Dühring), 8th Ed. Stuttgart, 1914, p. 342.—Marx, *Das Kapital*, I, 43, "We do not transform world problems into theological ones, but theological problems into worldly ones".

[40] *Deutsche Ideologie*, p. 22.

But in addition we must note that the production of these ideas is not a capricious process; nor can it be capriciously eliminated and thus not even by a prohibition of the State! The history of these ideas, if it is correctly written, is a history of the conditions which drive men towards them, and mirror themselves in them; they have no more an independent history of their own than, for example, the forms of law, a history which might be produced by men of genius, founders of religion, and saints.[41] So also Christianity has no history of its own, and "all the different forms in which it was expressed at different times were not . . ." further developments of the religious spirit, but were produced by entirely empirical causes remote from all influence of the religious spirit.[42] That in these ideas these conditions are reflected has a threefold significance. 1. The supernatural powers are mystifications of sociological dependences, masquerades of earthly conditions, but at the same time wear masks which correspond to the latter. The ways of thought and the conditions of a cultural period can be read off from them. The "forms of fantasy" are "representatives of forces of society".[43] 2. As a result of the struggle between man and nature they mark the gaps in contemporary knowledge and domination of nature, they are types of primitive pre-scientific explanation of nature. 3. The function of these ideas results, as does their content, from their conditioning causes; they are consolation, and indeed both a "moral sanction" and a "solemn completion" of the existing world. In the moral sanction those who profit from the existing order are interested; in the solemn completion all are interested, since all suffer from the existing order. Above all, the oppressed have recourse to this, and those who profit from it offer it to them in order to console them and to keep them quiet by its means. But since even those

[41] Ibid. pp. 23, 63.—Compare in contrast the account of Church history by Marx's Hegelianizing contemporary F. C. Baur, who emphasizes the history of ideas.

[42] Ibid. p. 152.

[43] *Anti-Dühring,* pp. 342f.

who profit from it are sufferers, they also have need of the consolation of religion. So religion is the universal ground of consolation and the ground of justification of the world as it is. "It is the fantastic realization of human nature, because human nature has no true reality. . . . The misery of religion is at one and the same time the *expression* of the real misery and also the *protest* against the real misery", but it is the latter in the same manner as the Chinese coolie reaches for the opium-pipe; it is "opium for the people".[44]

It belongs to the nature of forms created by fantasy, that they can be taken seriously and considered real only so long as their fantastic character is not seen through. The man who sees through it, is free from them. The enlightenment concerning religion prepares for its irrevocable end; liberation from religion is brought about by the enlightenment, which consists in scientific progress. In the case of religion, the sociological conditions of human life are its causes; it can be explained in terms of these, and it cannot stand up to its "genetic-critical" explanation.[45] But in this context it must be noted:

1. Enlightenment consists in the progress not only of the knowledge of nature, but also of the knowledge of history and above all in the knowledge of society, that is, the knowledge of the structural system of society and its laws which is brought by "historical materialism".

2. Enlightenment only brings real liberation, which can be greeted as liberation, and not deprecated as disappointment and deprivation, and therefore answered by a continually repeated reaching for the narcotic, when also the relations from which religion takes its rise are so changed that the need for sanctions and for consolation automatically disappears, and in consequence religion dies a natural death. "The mere

[44] K. Marx, *Einleitung zur Kritik der Hegelschen Rechtsphilosophie*, p. 208.
[45] Thus Feuerbach describes his programme as early as 1839. (See Bockmühl's book on Feuerbach and Marx, *Zeiblichkeit und Gesellschaft*, Göttingen, 1961, p. 69.)

knowledge is not sufficient to bring the social powers under the sovereignty of society. For this above all a social *act* is necessary. And when this act has been performed, when by the seizure of possession and the planned manipulation of the whole means of production, society has freed itself and all its members from the slavery in which they are at present held by these means of production, produced by themselves, but confronting them as a dominating alien power, when man no longer merely thinks, but also directs, only then will the last alien power which still today is reflected in religion disappear, and with it will disappear the religious reflection itself, for the simple reason that there will then be left nothing to reflect."[46] While in passing, we draw attention to the eschatological language in which such sentences are expressed, we observe that here we have not to deal merely with an intellectual enlightenment but, so to speak, a material enlightenment, which occurs when men increasingly discover that in the social changes brought about by themselves, they can bring under their feet, under their control, the powers which seemed to stand above them, and thus that nothing stands above them, but that everything is subject to them. But this in its turn presupposes that already previously, in the midst of the world of men who offer a religious interpretation, there are some enlightened men who already anticipate what is to come, who have already freed themselves from narcotics, because the future is their consolation, and, indeed, a really attainable future. They realize that the existing world is not the only possible one, not one that lasts for ever, not a necessary and inevitable form of human life, not an inescapable vale of woe, but one that "passes away" (I Cor. 7:31), which can be transcended, which is an alterable transitional condition. For them the future has become a practical challenge

[46] *Anti-Dühring*, pp. 344f.—The formula of the "last alien power" recalls in a significant manner the Pauline word about death as "the last enemy", that must be overcome I Cor. 15:26), with which the perspective is indicated, which Engels did not think of, and whose criterion he cannot escape!

to the present: "The challenge to give up the illusions about their condition, is the challenge to give up a condition which needs illusion."[47]

The significance of religion is here at once rated high and low; high in so far as the consolatory illusions dispensed by it hinder men from tackling the conditions themselves. Low, in so far as religion as a secondary phenomenon cannot have the dignity of a principal opponent. Because religion is only "a reflection of the social conditions"[48] Marxist atheism cannot be an end in itself, and the struggle against religion cannot be an independent task of socialism.[49] This distinguished Marx and Engels from the atheist thinkers on whom they base themselves, so far as the latter have "completed" the criticism of religion. It distinguishes them also from the young Hegelians who remained stuck in anti-theism,[50] as also from those socialists who make the struggle against religion a chief task of the socialist movement, thus turning it into an anti-religion,

[47] Marx, *Frühschriften,* p. 208.—In the Preface to his Dissertation he quotes the saying of Epicurus, "He is not wicked, who takes away the gods from the masses, but he who ascribes the honour of men to the gods". On the "presupposition" see also the even earlier A. Ruge, Works, 6, vol. 2: *Studien und Erinnerungen aus den Jahren 1843–1845* (Studies and Memories from the Years 1843–1845): "The German criticism of Christianity is the necessary presupposition of all liberation"—and E. Bauer, *Der Streit der Kritik mit Kirche und Staat,* Berne, 1844, p. 9: "The criticism of religion is the foundation of all further criticism". (Quoted from R. Seeger's book named on p. 15, note 4.)

[48] *Anti-Dühring,* p. 343.

[49] Cf. Marx (Paris manuscripts), *Frühschriften,* p. 237: "Communism begins at once (Owen) with atheism, but atheism is at first a long way from being Communism, since that atheism is much rather an abstraction." Page 248: "Atheism as denial of this unnecessary character has no longer a meaning, for atheism is a negation of God, and posits through this negation the being of man; but socialism as socialism no longer needs such mediation; it begins with the theoretically and practically sensuous consciousness of man and nature as of being. It is the positive self-consciousness of man, no longer mediated through the annulment of religion."

[50] In *Die heilige Familie,* Ausgabe des Dietz-Verlages, East Berlin, 1953, p. 232, it is said of Bruno Bauer: "He attacks the religious consciousness as an independent existence".

and deflecting it from the chief task of social change. For this reason Engels attacks Dühring,[51] and the efforts of the Bakunin group to make atheism obligatory for members of the workers' party.[52] It was thus, to adopt a distinction used in the language of the Communist party, meant in the "strategic" and not in the "tactical" sense, valid only for the moment, when Wilhelm Liebknecht called the well-known declaration of the Erfurt Programme of the S.P.D., "Religion is a private affair", "an utterance required only by practical considerations". "Instead of dissipating our powers on side-issues" (!) he said at the party conference in Halle in 1890, "we attack the economic basis on which the class-state of today, together with the Churches and Confessions and the parsons stand; if the basis collapses, then everything else falls with it."[53]

None the less, Liebknecht's qualification, that practical considerations are here at stake, and that the party has among all its claims no more practical proposition than this,[53a] betrays a certain inconsistency; these "side-issues" are by no means

---

[51] *Anti-Dühring*, p. 344: "Mr Dühring cannot wait until religion dies this natural death. He goes more to the root of things. He out-Bismarcks Bismarck; he decrees more extreme May laws, not only against Catholicism, but against all religion in general—he incites his policemen of the future against religion, and helps it to become a martyr, and to prolong its life. What are we thinking of?—particularly Prussian Socialism." Similarly in *Der Volksstaat* of 24.6.1874 ("On Religion", p. 115): "So much is certain; the only service that one can do to God in these days is this, to make atheism a compulsory article of faith, and go beyond Bismarck's laws of the Church-Cultural Struggle by forbidding religion altogether."

[52] Letter to W. Liebknecht of 31.12.1871.

[53] Protocol of the Party Conference in Halle, 1890, p. 202. Ibid. p. 197: "If we once have the Socialist State, we shall very easily make an end of religion"; p. 175: "Science ensures good schools, that is the best method against religion." Characteristic is also the famous word of August Bebel in his polemic against the chaplain Hohoff, which by its juxtaposition only conceals the inconsistency in the attitude to religion: "Christianity and Socialism are contrasted with each other as fire and water. We aim in the political field at the Republic, in the economic field at Socialism, and in what is today called the religious field, at atheism." Berlin, 1874.

[53a] *Protocol,* p. 197.

36

merely side-issues, if the critical unmasking of religion as the reflection of conditions of misery is "the presupposition of all other criticism", as we heard Marx say. A contradiction appears in Marx himself, when on one hand he can cast it in Feuerbach's teeth that he "still ascribes too much importance to the struggle against religion",[54] and on the other hand can set the social revolt as the goal of the criticism of religion. "Criticism has plucked the imaginary flowers on the chain, not in order that men may carry the forlorn chain, stripped of its fantasies, but that he may throw the chain away and pick living flowers. The criticism of religion disillusions man, so that he may think, act, and form his reality like a disillusioned man, a man who has come to his senses, in order that he may revolve round himself and his real sun".[55] As early as Feuerbach the declaration of the true, i.e. illusionary nature of religion, is both the presupposition and the task of progressive politics. At the beginning of his 24th Lecture on "the Nature of Religion" (1848–9), he declares himself sharply opposed to the "unconditional liberty to believe what one wishes. I retort in answer, that such conditions, when political freedom is linked to religious prejudice and narrowness, are not true conditions. For my part, I do not care a fig for political freedom, if I am a slave of my religious illusions and prejudices. True freedom is only present where a man is also free in religion, true education is only present where a man becomes the master of his religious prejudices and illusions. The goal of the State can be nothing less than the formation of the true, perfect man; a State whose citizens have free political institutions, but are not free in respect of religion, can therefore be no truly human and free State." The freedom for each man "to be saved in his own fashion" is therefore the "first condition of a free State", but it is also "a very subordinate and formal freedom, for it is nothing else than the

---

[54] *Deutsche Ideologie*, p. 242.
[55] "Einleitung zur Kritik der Hegelschen Rechtsphilosophie" in *Frühschriften*, p. 208.

freedom, or the right, of each man to be a fool at his own choice". However, the true "task of man in the State" is "not only to believe what one will, but to believe what is reasonable; in general, not only to believe, but also to know what he can and must know, if he is to be a free and educated man". Therefore the contemporary State, the State in the sense in which we have hitherto spoken of it, must refrain from all incursions into the field of faith, but—and now Feuerbach significantly does not go on to picture the behaviour of a future State when confronted by religious folly, but, evidently shrinking back himself from the idea of such anti-religious repression, he limits himself to speaking of the task of man in the State, and warning against underestimation of the harmful influence of religion on public life.

In a similar sense, in his criticism of the Gotha Programme (1875), Marx affirmed the slogan "Freedom of conscience" only in relation to the contemporary State. "Everyone must fulfil his religious as well as his bodily needs without the police sticking in their noses." But the party must in the same breath declare "that bourgeois 'freedom of conscience' is nothing but the toleration of all possible sorts of religious freedom of conscience, and that itself it rather seeks to free men's consciences from the spectre of religion."[56] In these utterances, in spite of all characteristic reserve, the perspective of a totalitarian state-power shows itself, which, through its superior, enlightened knowledge of what is "reasonable" encroaches upon the innermost conscience of its citizens, omniscient, controlling, and directing with a more gentle or more rigorous pressure.[57] It is the religious question which

[56] *Ueber die Religion,* p. 116.

[57] The Jacobinical undercurrent of European rationalism comes repeatedly to the surface, and confirms the words of Goethe's country minister (*Brief des Pastors zu *** an den neuen Pastor zu ****, 1773): "Nothing is more wretched than to let people hear unceasingly of reason, while at the same time they act only from prejudice. Nothing is so dear to them as tolerance, and their disdain at everything which is not their opinion, proves how little peace one can expect from them."

provides the decisive criterion of the self-limitation of power, and thus of its totalitarian character. The arrogance with which these rationalists sit in judgment on religion here becomes the arrogance exercised by man in relation to man in the name of reason, and it undertakes, in place of the exploitation of man by man in the name of property, to set up a not less shocking slavery. The whole history of Marxism and its political attitude to religion is characterized by the principle of this immanent self-contradiction; the one pole is the attempt to unite the workers in the practical goal of the revolution, and therefore to limit criticism of religion to the socially reactionary exploitation of religion, and dependence on the Church, the clergy, and so on, thus in principle to limit it to criticism of the Church, but for the rest to permit tolerance to prevail within the labour movement in metaphysical questions, and to resist attempts to bring the movement into subservience to the free-thinkers, and to make atheism obligatory. Because this restraint does not rest on real freedom from anti-religious dogma, but only on the conviction that religion is of secondary importance, and will die out in the future, the other pole is therefore the wish to free the workers from their religious "chains", because these hinder them from revolutionary thinking, and for this reason tolerance is only impatiently and unwillingly borne with, and for this reason Lenin declares the preaching of militant atheism to be an essential task of the party, for this reason the affirmations of tolerance in relation to the churches are made, broken, or limited according to the conditions of the hour. Apart from the political circumstances, the movement between these poles is connected with the life-history of the leaders; therefore with Marx and Engels the emphasis is stronger on the first pole, with Lenin, stronger on the second.

The Marxist theory of religion as a verdict upon religion becomes perfectly clear when we refer to the difference which obtains within its description of the world as "objective spirit"—or, in Marxist terms, of the "superstructure". The distinction between material basis and superstructure in the life of man in society, the question of the relations between the basis (the relations of production) and the phenomena of the superstructure in the life of man in society (law and politics together with the corresponding forms of consciousness), the secondary status of the latter, and the interplay of both, have for long been an inexhaustible theme of discussion in "historical materialism". If one adopts the schema, which is doubtless of great heuristic fruitfulness, but which has a certain *Weltanschauung* as its presupposition, then the assertion that religious ideas reflect social relationships does not necessarily commit one to a negative verdict upon the latter. That we men, even in regard to religion, use the language of our time, that consequently in our religious utterances the conditions of our time become visible, that social relationships recur in the language of religious metaphor, that the distresses and needs of society are also problems of religious life, and that, in conclusion, the interests of society try to take advantage of religious institutions and ideas—all this belongs to the phenomenology and sociology of religion, as it belongs to the phenomenology of law, of art, and so forth. Historical materialism as a reaction against an isolating manner of observation is the attempt to obtain a conspectus of all the territories of human life in their indivisible interdependence. So it is valid for *all* institutions, undertakings, and conceptions in the separate sectors of life, that they are produced by men in society, have no independent history, and provide ideological motives for social action.[58] If, however, the programme of ideological criticism is carried through, if "all the different products and forms of consciousness" are explained in terms of the "material production of immediate life", and consequently not "practice explained in terms of idea" but "the formation of ideas in terms of the

[58] *Deutsche Ideologie*, p. 36: "For example, an epoch imagines that it is determined by purely 'political' or 'religious' motives, although 'Religion' and 'Politics' are only disguises of their real motives."

material practice",[59] that has very different consequences for the phenomena of the different spheres of life, in so far as State, politics, law, and also morality, philosophy and art are not liquidated,[60] not they themselves but only the false consciousness connected with them being dissipated. Religion alone disappears as a territory, with all its ideas and activities. No objective realm, no reference to reality belongs to it, save that whose disclosure causes its death. This exception of religion from the other forms of the superstructure is important for two reasons. (1) The question about the reference of religion to reality leads to the question about the ontological presuppositions underlying the assertion of the "illusory" character of all religious ideas, and thus about the concept and criterion of "reality" which is here in use. (2) The different treatment of the individual forms of the superstructure indicates that the whole schema of basis and superstructure gives a semblance of unambiguity which on closer investigation it does not retain. The older Engels himself had his difficulties when he tried to determine in closer detail the effective relations of the two planes, and was no longer able to make the one-way causal schema work. Much later then the debate about the science of speech[61] disclosed that the dichotomy, which had first been subjected to the suggestion of the casual dualism of cause and effect, is inadequate, because there are phenomena in the life of the

[59] Ibid. pp. 34f.

[60] The "dying away" of the State in the Marxist prognosis is to be sharply distinguished from the "dying away" of religion; the State dies away in the Communist society of the future, because it loses its legitimate function. Religion dies away because it loses its illegitimate function; the former is a real process, the latter a rational one. The repeatedly discussed future fate of philosophy depends on the definition of what is understood as philosophy. On the sequence of the customary enumeration of forms of superstructure, politics, law, philosophy and theology, cf. M. Reding, *Der Politische Atheismus,* 1957, p. 257.

[61] Cf. J. Stalin, *Der Marximus und die Fragen der Sprachwissenschaft.* On this see my report, "Stalins Briefe zur Sprachwissenschaft", in *Eckart,* 1953, pp. 317–22.

41

spirit which cannot be fitted into this without remainder; for example those neutral cases which can neither be counted as belonging to the basis nor as belonging to the super-structure, and yet have a part in both, but which (in contrast with the entities of the superstructure) are to a considerable extent indifferent to changes in the basis. It was Stalin who established this in relation to language, and then at once in the Soviet discussion the concession was extended to mathe-matics and natural science; a limited rehabilitation of formal logic was added. The Soviet jurists did not omit to report from their field such neutral structures, in order to recover from that vantage point objective norms of law,[62] and no less did both Christian theologians and Marxist ideologists attempt to find a lodging-place for their disciplines in the realm of these "neutral factors". Historical materialism as an "exact science" "originated under capitalist conditions, but does not belong to the capitalist superstructure", declares George Klaus,[63] but, at the same time, he is of the opinion that it does not belong to the socialist superstructure, because, like the natural sciences it reflects "the objective reality", whereas all non-Marxist varieties of the social sciences are unable to resist their allocation to the super-structure: "All pre-Marxist theories about society are forms of the contemporary superstructure, and are liquidated along with it. They cannot serve different bases".[64] The Marxist theoretician only reveals by these sentences that he shares the old fate of the relativist; in order to assert his general relativism as the truth, he must make an exception in favour of his own standpoint, and posit it as absolute.

Apart from the *naïveté* of his procedure, however, even Klaus must distinguish between the general theories which he classifies thus, and "the facts and individual correct inferences

[62] Cf. the report on "Sozialistische Rechtstheorien" in *Ostprobleme*, 1953. IV, p. 147f.

[63] G. Klaus, *Jesuiten, Gott, Materie. Des Jesuitenpaters Wetter Revolte wider Vernunft und Wissenschaft, East Berlin*, 1958, p. 127.

[64] Ibid. p. 126.

used and co-ordinated in these theories", which do not fall a victim to liquidation; this means, however, that he has an awareness of the difference between a dogmatic function of scientific theories, in which these are transient, and their authentic scientific function, in which, in the process of scientific work they are always meant as provisional, as general projects, with the intention that they shall be improved upon. Klaus formulates as a general maxim "Only such theories are liquidated with the superstructure as do not adequately reflect the objective reality, but are only the ideology of the interests of the ruling class."[65] Thus a distinction is made according to the standard of a concept or reality which is judged to be unambiguous, a distinction which continually leads to true judgments. And there is a further distinction made between a mental activity and the objective realm co-ordinated with this activity on the one hand, and, on the other hand the theories and special forms which connect themselves with it in a particular class-situation. In the case of religion, however, such a distinction is ignored from the start, it is only "theory" in the pejorative sense, in the sense of deceptive ideology and illusion. Thus we come yet once again upon the presupposed concept of reality with which we must deal in the discussion between Christians and Marxists.

With the last arguments we have moved away from Marx in respect of history, but not in respect of the content of our theme. He proved his lack of interest in the theme of religion by his expounding as axiomatic the view of religion pictured above; nowhere is there to be found in him an attempt to give an independent and thorough systematic justification of it, and only superficially and occasionally does he illustrate it by individual observations. After his short intensive preoccupation with the phenomenon of religion through his reading of works on comparative religion, and giving a sketch of his own critical thoughts within the

[65] Ibid. p. 124.

framework of the work in preparation for his Dissertation,[66] Marx decisively turned his back on these problems. His statement "The criticism of religion is in the principle completed", sounds like the sigh of relief of a man who is glad that he is to be saved further trouble.

[66] Cf. the exact analysis by K. E. Bockmühl, *Leiblichkeit und Gesellschaft. Studien zur Religionskritik und Anthropologie im Frühwerk von L. Feuerbach und K. Marx*, Göttingen, 1961, pp. 110–56.

CHAPTER THREE

Ludwig Feuerbach's Criticism of Religion

IF one surveys the anti-Christian literature as it spread[1] in Germany before and after the Revolution of March 1848 under the shadow of the "most Christian State" and the "theological" Government of Frederick William IV (as the Bauer brothers were accustomed to express themselves), the irritated and peremptory character of the polemic strikes one. That Christianity is a spent force is regarded as beyond question, the nature of the concept of religion in general is not problematic, the hurtfulness and inhumanity of all forms of religion is continually demonstrated and at the same time regarded as an *a priori* presupposition. This kind of tone, so incongruous with the complex character of religious phenomena and the depth of the experience of the world which finds expression in them, is a reaction against the reality of the State Church, and therefore died down after its elimination. It has a similar spontaneity today only in lands with clerical régimes, and will continually revive where the tendency to such régimes is traceable. Where it is cultivated elsewhere, as for example in the anti-religious literature of the Soviets, we have to do with an inherited ritual which itself can only flourish behind the protective wall of a new "State Church" system. At that time, in the middle of the nineteenth century, the German bourgeoisie was divided in itself; it participated in the fruits of the revolutionary movement, and was at the same time anxious about its consequences; it needed for its evolution the dissolution of the

[1] Cf. K. Löwith, "Die philosophische Kritik der christlichen Religion im 19 Jahrhundert" in *Theologische Rundschau*, 1933, iii and iv, and "Ludwig Feuerbach und der Ausgang der klassischen deutschen Philosophie" in *Logos*, 1928, pp. 323f.

aristocratic world, and feared at the same time the mutterings of the new proletarian classes, who wanted to take advantage of this revolution and carry it further. The bourgeoisie found religion as the guarantee of the inherited order, and needed it as the guarantee of its own order. So bourgeois conservatism and bourgeois revolt are found side by side, and, mediating between them bourgeois liberalism, which could appear both as radicalism and as the confederate of Churchly convention.

While the rebellious criticism of the Young Hegelians was merely an affair of small intellectual circles, Ludwig Feuerbach's appearance found a remarkably strong response. His championship of nature and science, his appeal to the consciousness of progress, his sermonic tone, and the sentimentality of his new religion of love fitted very exactly the taste and needs of a class which created new economic facts, and which was therefore impressed only by facts, for which the advancement of science was a guarantee of its own advancement, and which in the stern struggle for profit wished yet to find a place for soul and kindly sentiment. For the educated members of this class, the great impression created by Feuerbach's criticism of religion was based on the fact that it could be regarded as a concentration of all previous efforts to liberate men from an ecclesiastical control which was resented as spiritual compulsion. Behind it stood both the Hegelian philosophy and the eighteenth-century criticism of religion from Spinoza down to the French materialists.

When Marx in 1844 states that the criticism of religion is in essence completed, that was both an acknowledgment of Feuerbach's achievement (he must have been thinking chiefly of him, although he was also greatly indebted to his Berlin associates in discussion, especially Friedrich Koeppen and Bruno Bauer).[2] At the same time it was a gentle

[2] For Koeppen cf. A. Cornu, *Karl Marx, L'homme at l'œuvre. De l'hégélianisme au matérialisme historique, 1818–1845,* Paris, 1934, p. 113; and Bockmühl, op. cit. p. 113; for Bruno Bauer cf. the preface of E. Barnikol to his edition of Bauer's *Das entdeckte Christentum.*

expression of surprise that Feuerbach still continued stead-fastly to concern himself with this settled matter. As a matter of fact, Feuerbach did this to the end of his life. In spite of his well-known self-description, "God was my first thought, reason my second, man my third and last thought",[3] he never freed himself from the contrast between his "first" thought and his "last"; he never saw his task of fighting against God for man "finished". "All his life long God tormented him", says Sergius Bulgakov of him.[4] We must attempt to outline his position, to which, with small varia-tions, he adhered to after his parting from Hegel.[5]

Two impelling motives become clear; an anti-idealistic concept of reality—and the wish to free man's concentration upon himself from every competing interest. As if a surfeit of spirit and a satiety with elevated abstraction had swung over to the other extreme, so the generation after Hegel sought reality where spirit appears only as a secondary phenomenon, in the material, in the perceptible and corporeal, in economics.

In his book *From Hegel to Nietzsche*,[5a] Karl Löwith

[3] *Sämtliche Werke* (later cited as *S.W.*), Leipzig, 1946, ff. vol. II, p. 410.

[4] Quoted by G. A. Wetter, *Der dialektische Materialismus,* p. 14, Marx's opposing thesis: "The religious questions of the day have today a *social* significance. There is no more talk of religious interests as such. Only theologians can believe that religion as religion is the matter of concern" (*Die heilige Familie,* p. 232), and, directly in opposition to Feuerbach's thesis, that the principal matter of concern for men had never been God, but only his predicates. "If now precisely the opposite of what Feuerbach said were the truth—and we make bold to say this—if neither God nor his predicates have ever been the principal concern of men, if this itself is only the religious illusion of the Germany theory . . ." *Deutsche Ideologie,* p. 239.

[5] Newer accounts: Schilling, *Feuerbach und die Religion,* Munich, 1957; G. Dicke, *Der Identitätsgedanke bei Feuerbach und Marx,* Cologne, 1960, and K. E. Bockmühl, *Leiblichkeit und Gesellschaft,* Göttingen, 1961. Cf. my review of the three works: "Verkündigung und Forschung" in *Theologisches Jahresbericht,* 1961–2, Munich, p. 239.

[5a] Ibid. p. 153.

has described in detail this transformation in intellectual history. As the epistemologies of Kant and Fichte expressed mistrust of sense-experience, so now there was a movement in the reverse direction, and a mistrust of the thought which attempts critically to transcend it. For this generation, which is moving towards the positivistic zeal for facts, it is precisely the resistance which non-intellectual being opposes to our conceptual powers, that testifies, as Löwith puts it, "like an incorruptible witness to the true being as the independent reality of an existent". In reaction to the intellectual reality of idealism, these younger men are gripped by the passion for the tangible, concrete, individual, perceptible, as the truly real, for the immediately visible as the really true. *"Indubitable, immediately certain,* is only what is *object of sense, of sight, of feeling."*[6] "Only the perceptible is clear as daylight. . . . The mystery of *immediate knowledge is sensation."*[7] "Only the senses give me . . . being."[8] Confronted by this "criterion of palpability"[9] it is clear that the whole field of religion cannot stand the test. "The object of perception is there *outside* of man; *the religious object is in him"*,[10] for "spiritual being is a being-thought, a being-believed."[11] There exist only sensible-palpable things, and ideas in the head; the first are real, the second unreal—the whole problem of reality, which previous philosophy had so unnecessarily complicated, all at once proved to be as simple as this.

Within this schema there were still variations according to whether the concept of the perceptible was understood more in the sense of the traditional epistemological inquiry as a description of the object presented to sense-perception—as Feuerbach largely took it—or whether the activity of man

[6] L. Feuerbach, "Grundsätze der Philosophie der Zukunft" in *S.W.*, vol. II, p. 326.   [7] Ibid. p. 326.
[8] "Das Wesen des Christentums", in *S.W.*, VII, p. 274.
[9] Thus the Hegelian K. Rosenkranz, quoted by Bockmühl, op. cit., p. 41.
[10] "Das Wesen des Christentums" in *S.W.*, VII, p. 38.
[11] Ibid. p. 273.

was included in it, so that it embraced the whole practical encounter of man with his world—as in Marx and Engels. The alternative character of the schema remains, it finds expression also in the basis-superstructure schema of historical materialism, and with it remains the simplification of the problem of reality. "The decision was taken to understand the real world—nature and history—in such a manner as it presents itself to everyone who approaches it without preconceived idealistic notions; the decision was taken to sacrifice mercilessly every idealistic notion which could not be brought into accord with things understood in their own context, and not in some fanciful context. And materialism means this and nothing more."[12] As if this were so simple! As if the whole history of philosophy hitherto had not arisen from the recognition of the difficulty of apprehending things as they are! The optimism of this programme of Engels corresponds to the optimism of his humanism, and makes one conjecture that this optimism is continually made possible only by simplifications which will at some time be found to disclose their illusory character.

The alternative presupposed by this schema is inadequate; it assumes the Cartesian conception of the subject-object relationship, and knows on the side of the *res cogitans* only ideas, which are produced by the human subject. The reality and power of psychic processes cannot be done justice to from this standpoint, religious statements and actions are understood only as theory on the plane of ideas, not as existential reactions and modes of behaviour in encounter with experiences of operative power. The sensation-philosophy and rationalism are united in Feuerbach; therefore he sees religious phenomena not as an expression both of the profundity of human nature and of the enigmatic and many-sided character of the world, but is able to believe that humanity will be "finished" with religion, as he, having seen

[12] F. Engels, *Ludwig Feuerbach und der Ausgang der klassischen deutschen Philosophie* (1888), Berlin, 1951, p. 37.

through it, had already finished with it. This is the belief of Marxism to the present day, that is one of its errors and a sign of its narrow-mindedness; for to have finished with religion is to have finished with man and the world, to have made them transparent, to have brought them under a manageable formula. The triumph of the man who thinks he has seen through religion is precisely the sign of his limitation, it is precisely he whom religion, whom the man of religion, has long since outdistanced with new surprises.

This schema of reality only shows its complete inadequacy when it is claimed to legitimate statements about the unreality of Christian language about God. Here it appears most clearly that a *metabasis eis allo genos* has occurred, in which an assertion in the realm of epistemology has been made into an ontological verdict.[13] That the assertions of Christian faith are not derived from sense-perception,[14] that consequently they cannot be empirically checked and verified by an "objective" observation; this has always been known by Christian thought, just as it has been known that the God of whom Christian faith speaks is not an existent alongside of other existents; that "being" and "reality" can be predicated of him only by the immediate application of a new and different determination of these concepts. Even the medieval Catholic doctrine of the *analogia entis* (analogy of being), in

[13] As G. Dicke rightly says, op. cit., p. 65: "Here we have a leap to the ontological plane—identifying again in a new manner the order of knowing and the order of being—which implies a tremendous constriction of reality."

[14] Nor are they derived from miracles, as Feuerbach, surely misled by an apologetic argument of ancient origin, repeatedly asserts, cf. "Pierre Bayle" in *S.W.*, VI, p. 50f., and "Ueber das Wunder" in *S.W.*, vol. I. He comes very much nearer to the problem with his assertion that there is a connection between miracle, and God's command and creative power, in contrast with the concept of a rigidly determined nature—so, e.g. "Das Wesen des Christentums" in *S.W.*, vol. VII, p. 179f.; 26th Lecture on "Das Wesen der Religion" in *S.W.*, vol. VIII, p. 304f., 24th Lecture, ibid. p. 287, "I believe in God means, I believe that there is no nature, no necessity".

spite of its problematic inclusion of Creator and creature in a common concept of being, sought to express the difference between divine and human being precisely by means of the concept of analogy.

Therefore it would not be right to blame either Schleiermacher or Hegel for the fact that Feuerbach has no consciousness of the differentiation of Christian language about the reality of God. When he made the assertion of the imperceptibility, and thus of the unreality of the object of religious ideas, and claimed that this was a new discovery of an overwhelming kind which lifted the Christian faith off its hinges, this can only, in my opinion, be understood as the expression of a new decision. What this group claimed to teach as a logically compelling discovery, was rather the assertion of a purpose, of a confession of faith. They wished to assure themselves of reality by insisting on its palpability to the senses, and therefore were able to discover beyond these limits only "ideas", whose reference to reality is decided by their reference to sense-perception.

It is difficult to decide whether the conception of God as an intolerable rival to the development of man was a consequence of this narrowing of the concept of reality, or whether the latter was a means of supporting the primary intention of excluding the divine competition. At any rate both motives offer each other mutual support.

1. If the passion for concrete corporeal reality regarded the idealistic conception of reality as an alienated and degenerate surrender to bloodless generalities, then God also fell a victim to this circumstance because he had long enough been subsumed under the concept of spirit and the idea. If idealism was a deflection that did not allow man to come to his reality, then God also was such a deflection. Faith in God fell a victim to the fate of metaphysical speculation, because it had for long enough been shored up by the latter.

2. If the primary aim was to win at last for man an unimpeded autonomy, then with the impeding authorities of

the feudal State, the Church, and the ordinances which the latter claimed had been divinely sanctioned, it was necessary for God, the so long cited metaphysical guarantor of these authorities, to fall also. His fall was, however, most certainly assured when a criterion of reality was set up which was accessible to everyone, and could be applied by everyone.

That in faith in God man is deceived about himself, that in order to win ourselves we must change ourselves "from candidates for the next world to students of this one,[15] this is the vehemently and monotonously asserted declaration of faith of the whole group from the Bauer brothers and Feuerbach to Marx. The whole of historical reality is forced on to this bed of Procrustes. Objections, instances to the contrary, self-revelations of those who, though Christian believers, ought to be able to judge as experts about the meaning and implications of their Confessional Statements, are disregarded, swept under the table, or misrepresented. Because it was so ordained from the beginning, therefore so it must remain, however much the experience of the people concerned contradicted it. "Where the heavenly life is a truth, there the earthly life is a lie."[16] "To leave everything as it is, that is the necessary consequence of the belief that a God rules the world, that everything happens and exists through God's will.[17] "The *emptier* life is, the *fuller*, the more concrete, is God. The emptying of the real world and the filling of the

[15] Concluding sentence from Feuerbach's Lectures on "Das Wesen der Religion" in *S.W.*, vol. VIII, p. 370. These lectures are intended to change the hearers "from friends of God to friends of man, from believers to thinkers, from men of prayer to workers, from candidates for the other world to students of this world, from Christians, who, by their own confession and admission, are '*half angels and half beasts*', to *men,* to *complete* men". Thus in Feuerbach's opinion, these are mutually exclusive opposites. "What is man—half beast, half angel", is a saying quoted by Friedrich Engels forty years later in his book on Feuerbach (op. cit. p. 24) as a favourite ideological slogan of the practical-materialistic philistine.

[16] "Das Wesen des Christentums" in *S.W.*, VII, p. 239.

[17] "Vorlesungen über das Wesen der Religion", op. cit., pp. 215ff.

Godhead is *one* act. Only the *poor* man has a *rich* God."[18] Whatever in such sayings sounds like an echo of Christian language, is robbed of its dialectic, so that a simple competition results between a vampire-like God and human development. How far the observation of the phenomenon of the decadence of religious life here plays a part is a question which the theologians in self-criticism should at once ask. It must here provisionally be set on one side, for a distinction between use and abuse, between right faith and decadence is precisely what is denied. What the defender of religion would like to claim was its decadence is here taken as its consequence and characteristic expression. This competitive relation is not the result of investigation but an axiom of criticism. All further analysis of religion serves only to confirm this axiom, which therefore is at the same time a principle of selection in the sifting of material which Feuerbach prepared for himself in extended historical studies dealing with theology, the Church, and the religions.

The resultant theory of religion indicates that all religion—the God of Christian faith is unhesitatingly reckoned as one of the gods of the religions—is a product of human need, and, what is more, of unsatisfied human need. "God is . . . a substitute for the *lost world*."[19] The limitations which are set for the individual man impel him to imagine for himself power, wisdom, etc., without limits, and thus to project himself as "absolute personality" into the supernatural sphere. Death makes him long for immortality. "If man did not die, if he lived for ever, if there were *no death*, then there would be *no religion* either."[20] God is important to man as a means to the

[18] "Wesen des Christentums", op. cit. p. 115, cf., K. Marx, Paris manuscripts, Marx, and Engels, Collected Essays, I, 3, pp. 83ff. "The more that man posits in God, the less he retains in himself."
[19] "Wesen des Christentums" op. cit., p. 268. Compare with this section the careful investigation in Bockmühl, op. cit. pp. 83ff.
[20] "Vorlesungen über das Wesen der Religion" op. cit., p. 41; but in a later passage (p. 360) Feuerbach objects to himself that man would also become tired of an eternal life, and then decides that man does not so much fear death in general as "the abnormal cases"—premature, violent and terrible death!

end of immortality, for "reason cannot satisfy this hope"; therefore the doctrine of the resurrection of Christ is *"the satisfied desire, the realized wish of man for immediate certainty of his personal survival after death".*[21] Finally the historical limitations, "the pressure of life, especially of civic and political life"[22] are added to the list. This is the point where K. Marx will interpose, in order to define more exactly the urge of man to reduplicate his world and secure his fulfilment in a religious world above. In his opinion Feuerbach performed the work of dissolving "the religious world down to its foundations. But the fact that the worldly foundation alienates itself from itself and creates for itself an independent kingdom in the clouds, is only to be explained from the self-fragmenting character and the inner contradictions of this earthly foundation. This itself must be understood in itself both in its contradiction and revolutionized in practice."[23] Finally what has the greatest significance for Feuerbach is the longing of man for love; both the longing to be loved and the longing to be able to love an object unquestionably worthy of love, so he creates in religion this possibility for himself by regarding himself "as a *divine object,* as a *divine goal;* for this reason the love of God to man is the *basis* and *centre of religion.*"[24]

Thus in religion man relates himself to himself, he is the producer, he is also the disguised object of these ideas. The study of religion does not disprove, but confirms that man himself is the centre, and that he is the total being that includes everything in itself. "All speculation about law, the will, freedom, personality without man, outside of man, or indeed above him, is a speculation *without unity, without necessity, without substance, without ground,* without reality. Man is the existence of freedom, the existence of personality, the exist-

[21] "Wesen des Christentums", op. cit. pp. 191f.
[22] Ibid. p. 191.
[23] *Frühschriften,* p. 340.
[24] "Wesen des Christentums", op. cit., p. 95.

54

ence of law. Man alone is the *ground* and *basis* of the Fichtean ego, the *ground* and *basis* of the Leibnizian monads, the *ground* and *basis* of the Absolute."[25] He is the subject, all the rest are his predicates. That is the conversion to which the statements of theology, as of philosophy, must be subjected in order to bring their content to light.

In religion we have to do with man himself. Its origin lies in human egoism. But this is not the reprehensible thing in it; but that it is a wrong way to satisfy human need, which hinders man from seeking to fulfil it in the right way. That it is a wrong way is certain if only because of its unreality. For Feuerbach the pragmatist idea of the beneficial illusion is impossible. The untruth of religion necessarily implies its harmfulness.

1. If man makes himself a predicate of his predicate, then in the self-abasement of this abstraction he is untrue both to his dignity and to his bodily nature; he regards and treats himself, together with nature, to which he belongs, as something inferior, in order to gain a supposedly more valuable spirituality. This is supported by a full but tendentious selection of instance from church history and comparative religion.[26]

2. The true perfection, as whose false representative man has fabricated God and the gods, is given to him in the species of mankind. We feel ourselves morally, materially, spatially and temporally limited, therefore "Where shall we redeem ourselves from this feeling of limitation, if not in the thought of the unlimited species, i.e. in the thought of other men, other places, other happier times? He who therefore does not set the species in the place of the Deity, leaves a gap in the individual which necessarily is filled again by the idea of a God, i.e. a personified idea of the species. Only the species is in a position both to eliminate and to replace the

---

[25] *S.W.*, vol. II, p. 267.

[26] In this respect Feuerbach belongs to the movement principally represented by the young Heine, who contrasts "the rehabilitation of the flesh" with a Christianity reduced to its ascetic tendencies.

Deity and religion."[27] Here Feuerbach finds the real immortality, omniscience and blessedness, the compensation of his limitation and imperfection, even the true forgiveness of sins.[28] The species is, however, completely and really represented only by the "Thou" of our fellow-man. Idealism was a "monologue of the solitary thinker with himself"[29]; the basis of its thought was the isolated individual, even when it spoke of spirit, and it could reach the elimination of solitude only in a dialectic which started from the thought of the solitary spirit, and concluded with it once more. The real elimination of solitude is given in the confrontation of "I" and "Thou", from which religion and metaphysics lure me away, in order to let myself be enslaved by an individualistic and solitary search for salvation.

In the reduction of Christianity to spirituality and individualism the antipathy of the critic and the ballast of an old and questionable tradition reinforce one another. In making this verdict Feuerbach had no idea how near his insistence on our physical nature and our shared humanity had brought him to the structures of the biblical doctrine of man. A thick veil concealed this knowledge from him, and disastrously affected his own thinking. For neither was he able adequately to define the relation between our bodily nature and our shared humanity in its ethical significance (this, too, may have been the reason why Marx felt himself repelled by Feuerbach's sermonizing about love[30]), nor was he able to define the rela-

---

[27] *S.W.*, vol. I, pp. 351f.

[28] Op. cit., p. 222. "If I alone am the species, if apart from me there exist no other, qualitatively other men, or, what is absolutely the same, if there is no difference between me and the others, if we are all perfectly alike, if my sins are not neutralized and deadened by the opposed characteristics of other men; then indeed my sin is a disgrace that cries to heaven, a shocking horror, which can only be effaced by extraordinary, superhuman miraculous means."

[29] Collected Works (*S.W.*), vol. 2, p. 345. "The *true* dialectic is *no* monologue *of the solitary thinker with himself*, it is a *dialogue between I and Thou.*"

[30] Feuerbach's Dissertation: "On the One, Universal, Unlimited Reason", p. 47: *ipse ego omnes sum homines*—I myself am all men.

tion between our fellow-man and the species. After 1841 he did indeed avoid mentioning the concept of the species, but this was no answer to the problem as to who should take over the functions which had previously been ascribed to the species. He adhered without change to the idea of a total human self-realization which stood in need of no supplementation, and was subject to no questions or inner threats. This he saw as a harmony between our bodily nature and our shared humanity, but he never reflected on the explosive force latent in this word "and", but disguised it with panegyrics about true happiness in friendship and love. It is just here that we see that Feuerbach never sufficiently won clear of the influence of his pantheistic beginnings. As consistently from the start he understood Hegel in a pantheistic sense, so he himself began his career with a pantheistic mysticism of the unity of the finite and the infinite. And so death, which as the end of individuality, is yet at the same time the power also which most deeply stamps upon us our individuality, is interpreted by him as the elimination of the selfish existence, that insists upon its individuality, by the all-consuming love of God. "Perhaps it is possible that you, as this particular being, are nothing more than a moment of the infinite being"; so he writes in his early publication *Thoughts on Death and Immortality*.[31] This "infinite being" is then transformed into the "species". Participating in the species, man is not a particular being as is the brute, which is only an example of its species; he is rather "a member of the species", i.e. in such participation, a "universal being, not limited and unfree, but unlimited and free".[32] This is in essence only a transformation of the thesis in the still strongly Hegelian Dissertation *"De ratione una, universali, infinita"* of 1828; I am myself all men; *ipse ego omnes sum homines.* The pantheism is retained, "The

[31] *Gedanken über Tod und Unsterblichkeit aus den Papieren eines Denkers nebst einem Anhang theologisch-satyrischer Xenien, herausgegeben von einem seiner Freunde.* Nürnberg, 1830, p. 51.
[32] *Grundsätze der Philosophie der Zukunft* ("Fundamental Principles of the Philosophy of the Future"), *S.W.*, vol. 2, p. 342.

'atheism' is pantheism in reverse".[33] Thus the problem of individuation was never fully grasped by Feuerbach; the personal character of the I-Thou relationship—in spite of the fruitful suggestions which he passed on to others by using it[34] —was not apprehended in its particularity. This was a momentous failure, for pantheism applied to society is collectivism. Marxism has never succeeded in giving a clear definition of the contrast between the individual and society. It has not really recognized the personality of man; therefore it possesses no adequate picture of the role of the individual in the coming society—is the individual in Marxism reduced to a function of society, or is he there set free to enjoy his own existence?—Therefore the individual, as historical experience has since shown, is not protected from being regarded and treated as "nothing more than a moment in the infinite being of the collective". All this can be traced to Feuerbach's failure. "Every pantheistic tendency destroys with the independence and the person of God the independence and the person of man", rightly says Theodor Steinbüchel in his book on Ferdinand Ebner, who in the twentieth century realized anew and more decisively underlined the significance of the I-Thou relationship.[35]

The cause why Feuerbach was not able to do this, and therefore passed on to Marx such a fatal inheritance, lies in his atheism. Now the species had to take the place of the "imaginary counterpart", God. But as an abstract concept

[33] "Vorläufige Thesen zur Reform der Philosophie," Collected Works, vol. 2, p. 246.—Rudolf Lorenz has demonstrated this origin in a pantheistic mysticism "Zum Ursprung der Religionstheorie Ludwig Feuerbachs" in *Evangelische Theologie*, Munich, 1957, p. 171f.

[34] Cf. M. Buber, *Das Problem des Menschen,* Heidelberg, 1952, p. 62. "Feuerbach initiated that discovery of the 'Thou', which has been called the 'Copernican deed' of modern thought, and an 'elemental event'. It has just been as momentous as the discovery of the 'I' by Idealism, and must lead to a second new beginning of European thinking, which refers us beyond the first Cartesian entry of the newer philosophy. He gave me myself in the days of my youth the decisive stimulus."

[35] *Der Umbruch des Denkens,* 1937, p. 72.

58

the species is not fitted to do this. Or else the individual fellow-man, who as such is no more a universal being than the species, and can give no totality to the fellowship with him. Or else—in Marx—society, which, likewise, can only fulfil on paper the task which is laid upon it. Feuerbach and Marx were well aware that the man who hitherto had sought in fellowship with God his fulfilment, must pass through a stage of "disappointment" until he realizes where a real fulfilment beckons to him instead of a fictitious one. They were confident that reason would lead man to retire modestly within the boundaries of his own individuality which he longed to transcend in religion, and would make more palatable to him the participation in the social totality as a better fulfilment. For not resignation, but the triumph of fulfilment should be the final condition for society and for individual, to which the painful disappointment that there was no God was only the inevitable transition. Now an immanent quality of goodness must be ascribed to the finite, which, bereft of all other prospects, it does not possess—and an achievement required of it, of which it is not capable. "The restoration of a total and immediate identity of individual and society founders upon the impossibility of bringing the finite to completion by its own efforts. The finite is not capable of totality. The infinity . . . which is to be eliminated, appears in the finite as an endless bad infinity."[36]

Before we turn once again to Marxism, some more remarks must be included, as contributions to the theological discussion with Feuerbach.[37] The limits of Feuerbach's theory of religion can be quickly recognized:

1. The concept of religion as a unity is applied entirely without differentiation; all religions are subsumed under

[36] Thus states G. Rohrmoser, rightly: "Die Religionskritik von Karl Marx im Blickpunkt der Hegelschen Religionsphilosophie, in *Neue Zeitschrift für systematische Theologie,* 1960, p. 60.

[37] A review of the Feuerbach-discussion in Protestant Philosophy of Religion is given by the otherwise unfortunately inadequate book of W. Schilling, *Feuerbach und die Religion,* Munich, 1957, pp. 31–45.

theism, in order to provide a clear boundary between it and atheism, which in reality cannot be drawn in Comparative Religion.[38] And this in turn comes from the fact that Feuerbach's model, and the object of his polemic is, fundamentally and exclusively, Christianity. The refusal to distinguish between the God of Christian faith and the gods, and even to give consideration, as to a relevant theme, to the antithesis which runs through the Bible between God and the gods, is both the fault of the contemporary theology and the consequence of an intention to degrade Christianity. Only in the work of his old age, the *Theogony* (1857) does Feuerbach make the attempt to determine the relationship of Christianity to the other religions within the evolution of the history of mankind.

2. Within this concentration on Christianity Feuerbach certainly made well-informed and acute interpretations, and understood the significance of Christology better than did some theologians of his time. By his special attention (following Hegel) to Lutheran Christology, and here particularly to the statements which express God's condescension to man, he was able to reverse the formula *Deus homini homo* (God is a man for man) to *homo homini Deus* (Man is God to man), the "motto and outcome of his thought".[39] From the same interest, however, he neglected those sayings which speak of God's otherness, and of this as his holiness which judges men, and which consequently cannot be so easily fitted into the schema of wish-projection, but indicate that other experiences are under our scrutiny. This is true in the sphere of the philosophy of religion, as Rudolf Otto has shown, for the

[38] Cf. W. Trillhaas, *Der Atheismus* (*Ein Ueberblick*), in *Neue Zeitschrift f. syst. Theologie*, 1960, pp. 248–61; Karl Barth has therefore referred to the tendency of Atheism and Mysticism to pass the one into the other. *Kirchliche Dogmatik* I, 2, pp. 350–6. E.T., pp. 320–5.

[39] So Theodor Steinbüchel, *Sozialismus*, p. 45—the wording is, *Das Wesen des Christentums*, op. cit., p. 361: "*Homo homini deus est*, this is the turning-point of world history".

experiences of the *mysterium tremendum* (fearful mystery) which find expression in the distorted character of some pictures of the gods, by which indeed the gods are set apart from that which is wished for by man. In these is shown that here motives are still at work which cannot be subsumed under the concept of need, wish, and natural explanation. Feuerbach touches on this, since he also has to deal with sacrifice in religion. But he gives it too small a place in his interpretation as a result of his rationalistic psychology. "Denial is only one form of self-affirmation, of self-love. The point where this becomes most evident in religion, is *sacrifice*."[40]

3. Very closely connected with this is the fact that Feuerbach never gets beyond a eudaemonistic ersatz-religion. He does not, indeed, omit to refer to Kant's separation of religion from morality,[41] but for the rest he shares in a remarkable neglect of Kant, before whom the great form of Hegel had interposed itself, so that Kant's criticism of the ethic of the Enlightenment, and the unconditional character of the ethical imperative sank into oblivion. But it is highly questionable whether the knowledge of this unconditional character would have been possible without the Christian message which preceded it, without the reformed doctrine of the holiness of the divine law, and without the Christian view of man as the image of God. From an analysis of "The Fundamental Principles of the Metaphysic of Morals", this Christian basis of Kant, of which he himself was only dimly conscious, could be clearly indicated. But when God is removed, there the unconditional character of moral obligation collapses also, and the categories of the good and the useful are again confused, as is the case in Communist ethics up to the present day.

[40] End of the 8th Lecture on "Das Wesen der Religion", after which the 9th Lecture deals with sacrifice, and its "egoistic goal and ground" (*S.W.*, vol. 8, pp. 86ff).

[41] E.g. as early as in "Pierre Bayle", Collected Works, vol. 6, pp. 100ff.

4. As already mentioned, the genial certainty with which Feuerbach is accustomed to express himself is nowhere backed by real proof, the "nothing more than . . ." of his reductions relies on the suggestive effect of breath-taking disclosures, but on closer examination is seen never to get beyond the level of assertion. Feuerbach loves to lay down the law. The historical material does not serve to prove, but merely to illustrate the theses which were unquestioned from the beginning. The decision has been taken before he reaches for his pen, religion can be nothing more than illusion—and his work is only to show that as such it is not by any means a foolish or deceptive illusion, as the old rationalists had thought, but that there is a meaning in it, although admittedly a special meaning, one quite different from that which religious believers think. In this, Feuerbach's concept of projection is particularly specious. He acquired it in his discussion with Hegel, in his discovery of man as the concrete subject of spirit, old answers to the question about the origin of the idea of the gods are elaborated by it—for example, *timor fecit deos* (fear made (created) the gods), and the like. Feuerbach makes full use of its application, and backs it up with more far-reaching psychological reflections, and at the same time gives the concept a self-evident character which it does not naturally have in itself; the suspicion as such is reckoned to be the proof, the correspondence of Christian words such as grace, forgiveness and love with human needs (and thus the positive meaningfulness of these promises?) is for Feuerbach's unmasking zeal already the proof that they were produced *by* human need. The fact that faith consoles the man who was in need of consolation, is for him a sufficient proof that the need for consolation was its productive cause. Eduard von Hartmann long ago said the necessary word about this inference from correspondence to non-existence. "If the gods are wish-beings, absolutely nothing to prove their existence or non-existence follows from that."[42]

[42] *Geschichte der Metaphysik*, Leipzig, 1906, vol. 2, p. 444. "His only

Feuerbach's great achievement was to have shown that the religions were human self-expressions—not without precedent, but drawing the conclusions implied by earlier philosophy and theology, but with greater energy, persistence, and psychological sensitiveness. The man who, as a hearer of the Christian message, has his existence in that realm which is the target of Feuerbach's polemic, will indeed be ever anew overcome by the feeling of an unconscious folly disguised as arrogance, in his, as in Marx's utterances about religion; but he will do harm to his own cause if he gives in to it, and stops his ears against this criticism. The one-sidedness with which here—in contrast with the one-sided praises of religion by its apologists—the darker side and the deviations of the religious life are described as its essential expression, is by no means an indication of the lack of substance in the attack. The question posed by Feuerbach to theology was for long poohpoohed, but first underlined this century by Kurt Leese,[43] and then taken seriously by Karl Barth.[44] This question does not consist in asking whether theology can succeed in proving the objective reality of God and the Christian revelation. The problem of such a challenge is indeed only a part of the general problem of the epistemological dispute about the demonstrability of the reality of the external world. (Here the Marxist reference to practice and the Leninist theory of models gives no better a solution to the problem than

---

original thought is that the gods are human wish-projections. Now it is quite true that something does not exist, just because it is wished for, but it is not true, that something cannot exist, because it is wished for. Feuerbach's whole criticism of religion and the whole proof of his atheism rests however on this single inference, i.e. upon a logical fallacy. If the gods are wish-beings, absolutely no inference to their existence or non-existence can be made from this premise."

[43] *Die Prinzipienlehre der neueren systematischen Theologie im Lichte der Kritik Feuerbachs,* Leipzig, 1912.

[44] "Ludwig Feuerbach", in *Zwischen den Zeiten,* Munich, 1927, pp. 11–40, reprinted in *Die Theologie und die Kirche,* 1928, pp. 212–39, cf. also the chapter on Feuerbach in Karl Barth, *From Rousseau to Ritchl,* pp. 354–61.

Alexander gave to the problem of the Gordian knot!) A pan-illusionist theory of knowledge (Berkeley) is irrefutable, as is known, but it can be criticized by asking how a definite statement of the problem leads, not by intention, but by consequence, to such solipsistic idealism.[45]

In Feuerbach's case that means: if the empirical verification by the senses is set up as a criterion for the reference to reality of an idea, after the manner of the methods of the natural sciences, the necessary consequence in the case of religious ideas will follow that they are illusory—but only then. Theology faces then the problem of the verification of the contents of faith; the persistent application of that "criterion of tangibility" does it the service of making it conscious that its statements are completely unverifiable on *this* level. Yet this unverifiability was already implicit in the Christian confession that God is invisible, and that the Christian relationship to God is a matter of faith, and that there is a contradiction between "the cross" and "the flesh". Whether theology succeeds better in locating this verification on another level, and wherein this verification consists, for which alone it is possible on faith's presuppositions to hope, is a principal problem of the contemporary theological discussion and a permanent question of all Christian theology.[46] In order to refute the adequacy of this criterion in its own case, it is important for theology that the inadequacy of this criterion in the realm of philosophy also should be disclosed.

The question for Christian theology cannot therefore be how it can entirely remove faith from the suspicion of being illusory. That is just what it cannot do. For this reason, deeper and more all-embracing interpretations of religious pheno-

[45] Cf. K. R. Popper, "Das Problem der Nichtwiderlegbarkeit von Philosophien", in *Deutsche Universitätzeitung*, 1958.

[46] Compare on this point W. Matthias, "Ueber die anthropologische Verifizierung theologischer Begriffe" in *Ev Th.*, October, 1961, and, as for the questions concerned in all this discussion—Hans J. Iwand, *Glauben und Wissen*, Munich, 1961, vol. I.

mena, such as stem from Rudolf Otto and C. G. Jung, are at best improvements on the same level, which make no fundamental difference for theology. The question for theology can only be whether in the pursuit of its own concern to the best of its abilities it encourages and confirms this suspicion, or what answer on its own presuppositions it has to give to it. It is possible for it so to describe Christian faith—on apologetic grounds, in order to remove its offence, or because of its own dependence on a presupposed philosophical system, or because it has itself already confused faith with religious experience—that Feuerbach can with good reason call his theory of religion the consequence of such theology, or the disclosure of the real heart of the matter. This is always the result when theology—perhaps to avoid objectifying language about God, or in order to prove to outsiders the legitimacy and reality of faith—regards the consciousness of God as a necessary aspect of self-consciousness, and extols faith as the noblest development of a possibility present in man, the Christian message as the reputedly highest result of the historical development of ideas, or faith as a manner of existence visible and to be recommended in itself, i.e. in abstraction from the phenomenon of Jesus Christ. In all such cases it shrinks from confessing its dependence upon the underivably positive character of revelation, a character which cannot be understood from general principles. This the young Marx recognized acutely as the real cause of offence, when he described religion as the "sanction of the positive".[47] So long as theology, in order to secure its place in cultural life, represents faith as the realization of a possibility which can be generally perceived, it is powerless against the Feuerbachian

[47] Marx and Engels: Collected Essays I, 1, p. 160; cf. Bockmühl op. cit. pp. 145f.—Marx says: "the *universal* sanction of the positive" and implies by this as a necessary consequence, that because of the positive character of revelation, theology must everywhere challenge the autonomy of reason, and sanction the positive dogmas of unreason—a very often realized, but by no means necessary consequence, and one that always is evidence of bad theology.

reduction of the relation to God into the production of man for the satisfaction of a general need. "Man is the beginning of religion, man the centre of religion, man the end of religion."[48] It is then no longer of decisive importance whether this need is valued positively as something belonging to the perfection of human existence, or negatively as something hindering man's true perfecting, whether it is taken at its face-value, or as a disguised need, as a phenomenon arising from the repression of a deeper, more genuine need, in the manner of Feuerbach, Marx, or Freud. In that case it is established with the agreement of theology, that man is the valuer, and that what we have to do with is a subjectivism of values, and that God is not here origin and end, but a means to an end. In this manner theology runs into Feuerbach's net, and lets him demonstrate to it that its house, erected on human possibility, is built on a morass.[49] Thus theology can only confront the suspicion of its illusory character by *not* undertaking to refute it (for to do this would be to subject itself to empirical criteria of reality), or to eliminate that suspicion by a metaphysic of transcendence which, as the way from idealism to Feuerbach and Marx shows, instead of repelling it will only confirm it. Theology can only confront this suspicion with the daring with which it confesses to revelation, and exhibits the latter's peculiar quality, because only the word of revelation can itself give the confirmation of itself in the word of address which encounters the hearer. In the service given in this confession, it can demonstrate the dogmatic character of the suspicion of illusion. It can do so at that point where the suspicion becomes a general verdict, and—to speak with Charles Peguy[50]—faith can on its side unmask this suspicion as a "metaphysic of the modern world, that wishes to be

[48] "Das Wesen des Christentums", op. cit. p. 253.
[49] This objection must also be made to Marcel Reding's attempt within the framework of traditional Catholic Apologetic, to prove the belief in the Creator through the human need to find a causal explanation. (*Der politische Atheismus*, Graz, 1957, p. 318.)
[50] Quoted in *Hochland*, December 1949, p. 107.

physics". And thus it can drive it back to the situation where the question is still held open, which is the suspicion's true function. In doing this service to this confession, theology must not shrink from its proximity to religion, but it must also never identify its theme, the theme of the revelation of the living God, with religion. It will allow itself to be driven back by Feuerbach's question to its own position, and repent at the place where it is forced to discover that it has become subject to Feuerbach's verdict. Thus it will be forced to acknowledge in the criticism of Feuerbach and Marx an event of fundamentally positive significance for itself.[51]

[51] Kierkegaard was surely thinking along the same lines when he noted in his Diaries—"The revolution is actually nearer than people think. The latest band of freethinkers has made a much better attack or got a much better grasp of things than previously: if you examine closely you will see that they have actually taken over the job of defending Christianity against the Christians living today. The fact is that the Christian forces today are demoralized, people have lost all respect, in the deepest sense, for the existential obligations of Christianity. Now Feuerbach says 'No, stop! If I am to be permitted to live as I live, then I must also confess that I am not a Christian. . . .' He praises the Christians, in order to show that their life does not correspond to the teachings of Christianity. It may well be the case that he is a malicious demon, but as a matter of fact he is a useful figure" (Pap. X, 2, p. 163). For the Christian debate with Feuerbach I may further mention two essays of the Prague theologian J. M. Lochmann, which are in agreement with the viewpoint here expressed. They are "Von der Religion zum Menschen" in "Antwort", *Festschrift zu K. Barths 70 Geburtstag,* Zürich, 1956, pp. 596–709, and "Der Atheismus- Frage an die Kirche", *Ev. Th.,* March, 1958.

CHAPTER FOUR

The Problem of Immanent Eschatology in Karl Marx

MARX and Engels took over Feuerbach's criticism of religion uncritically, lock, stock and barrel. "Man makes religion, religion does not make man",[1] there was no change on this point. Their critical changes did not affect the content, but the limits of Feuerbach's thought, his omission of dialectic, his undialectical and still abstract description of man as the subject of religion. If the older Marx dealt ironically with the Feuerbach cult of his youth, still the way which as a young man he had so enthusiastically praised, had been an inevitable one for him. "And to you, speculative theologians and philosophers, I give this counsel, make yourselves free from the concepts and prejudices of speculative philosophy hitherto, if you wish to approach things as they are in a different manner, i.e. if you wish to come to the truth. And there is no other way for you to truth and freedom than through the fire-stream (Feuer-bach). Feuerbach is the purgatory of the present day."[2] Feuerbach holds this place also within the Marxist system, his reversal of subject and predicate in religion is a door through which all must pass. "Religion is in its essence the emptying of man and nature of all content, and the transference of this content to the phantom of a transcendent God, who then, in turn in his grace, lets some of his superfluity come to man and to nature." "*We* proclaim the content of history, but we see in history not the revelation of God, but of man. We do not need first to imprint the truly human with the stamp of the divine, in order to be certain of its great-

[1] *Frühschriften*, p. 207.
[2] MEGA I, 1, pp. 174f., *Luther als Schiedsrichter zwischen Strauss und Feuerbach*.

ness and glory. The question has hitherto been 'What is God?' And the philosophers have given this answer to the question, 'God is man. Man has only to know himself, to measure all the conditions of life by himself, to judge them according to his own being, to organize the world in a truly human manner according to the demands of his nature, and he has solved the riddle of our time.' " So writes the young Engels in 1844 in his essay on Carlyle,[3] and this fundamental tone persists. The last sentence, however, shows how far already these younger men are pressing on beyond Feuerbach; Feuerbachian man is himself an abstraction. He is conceived unhistorically, he is a timeless idea. For this reason Feuerbach's discussions about the causes of the religious perversion are inadequate, and therefore liberation from the latter, the conversion in Feuerbach, is still only an act of consciousness, an appeal to human honesty and motivated by reverence for human dignity. Because the thinking is unhistorical, it is therefore also conceived undialectically, his self-liberation is expressed in moral antitheses, and ends with an immediate self-identity, beyond which Feuerbach has nothing more to say than a vague eulogy of the bodily and of love, because he had forgotten the dialectic of the relations between man and his productions, between subjective and objective spirit, between the spirit and work, of which he had read in Hegel. Marx's new recourse to Hegel, which cannot here be described in detail,[4] makes it possible for him to replace the psychologico-genetic explanation of the origin of religion by a sociologico-genetic one, and this in the service of a revolutionary programme of action aimed at the overcoming of social conditions which make religion possible and necessary.

[3] MEGA I, 2, pp. 424, 427, 428.
[4] Compare on this point, in addition to the above-mentioned works of Bockmühl and Rohrmoser, H. Popitz *Der entfremdete Mensch. Zeitkritik und Geschichtsphilosophie des jungen Marx,* Basle, 1953; L. Landgrebe "Hegel und Marx", in *Marxismusstudien,* 1st Series, 1954, pp. 39–53, and I. Fetscher "Das Verhältnis des Malxismus zu Hegel" in *Marxismusstudien,* 3rd Series, 1960, pp. 66–169.

So this all takes place within the framework of an immanent eschatology, of which there is no trace in Feuerbach, for whom "The I-Thou relationship fulfils itself essentially in the present here and now. But Marx's deductions from the existential criticism of Hegel transcend the present both radically and decisively in favour and in respect of a distant goal'.[5] For this reason the criticism of religion, Feuerbach's central theme all his life long, now moves to the circumference. Because he had taken more seriously the question about the causes which drive men to religious projection, Marx thinks that he is able to give a better consolation to men disillusioned by criticism than Feuerbach was able to provide, and, therefore, that he can give them more courage to renounce the illusory consolations of religion. "It is an illusion of Feuerbach's that the destruction of an illusion could make mankind happy, and this gives the Feuerbachian humanism a Utopian character."[6]

It may in passing be observed that Feuerbach had in fact cast a glance in this direction; a fact which on the Marxist side is willingly passed over because of his political inactivity. He was indeed a bourgeois through and through, but he did not omit to notice that when the life for heaven is replaced by a life for earth, then work must replace prayer, and politics must replace religion: "For we *must* become religious again —*politics* must become our religion—but that it can only do, if we have a highest target in our sights, which makes politics into religion."[7] "The denial of the world beyond has the affirmation of this world as its consequence; the elimination

[5] Thus Thier, in the excellent introduction to his edition of the Paris manuscripts, *Karl Marx, Nationalökonomie und Philosophie*, Cologne, 1950, p. 31—*Das Menschenbild des jungen Marx*, Göttingen, 1957, p. 5.

[6] G. Kaus, op. cit. p. 54.

[7] *Ludwig Feuerbach in seinem Briefwechsel und Nachlass sowie in seiner philosophischen Charakterentwicklung*, Ed. K. Grün, vol. I, 1874, p. 409—This remark about the "highest" shows more clearly than the nervous avoidance of all religious terms on the marxist side the religious (let us not prematurely say the pseudo-religious!) background of the marxist talk of man as the highest being for man!

of a better life in heaven involves the challenge that things should and must become better on earth; it transforms this better condition from the object of an idle and inactive faith into an object of duty, of the activity of the human self."[8] Thus Karl Löwith is right. "With the same consistency as Kierkegaard explains the increased political activity of the times as a result of the decay of Christian faith, Feuerbach reasons to the necessity of political action as resulting from the faith in man as such."[9] Moses Hess does not, as he and Marx believed, draw this consequence from what was merely implicit in Feuerbach, but expresses more directly what was Feuerbach's own opinion, especially in his later years, when he says: "Feuerbach says the nature of God is the transcendent nature of man. . . . Theology is anthropology—that is true—but that is not the whole truth. We must add that the nature of man is his nature in society . . . and the true doctrine of man, the true humanism, is the doctrine of the ordering of society, i.e. anthropology is socialism."[10]

But this does not mitigate the repudiation of religion, it only sharpens it. What is at stake is nothing less than its annihilation.[11] "We have not to deal with its negative characteristics, where it prevails, there inhumanity, bondage, self-deception and self-seeking prevail. That the free, and at the same time social, man, who is to be created by the revolutionary development, must and will be an irreligious man,

[8] "Vorlesungen uber das Wesen Religion", Collected Works, vol. 8, p. 368   [9] *Von Hegel zu Nietzsche*, p. 95.
[10] Quoted in M. G. Lange's preface to his edition of Feuerbach, *Kleine Philosophischen Schriften*, East Berlin, 1950, p. 86.
[11] In the Paris manuscripts, *Frühschriften*, p. 278: "When I know religion as estranged human self-consciousness, I do not know in it as religion the confirmation of my self-consciousness, but the confirmation of my estranged self-consciousness. Thus I do not know in religion the confirmation of my self-consciousness which belongs to itself, to its own nature, but rather the confirmation of the annihilation and annulment of religion." Some years later in a review of G. F. Daumer's *Die Religion des neuen Weltalters*, 1850, in *Ueber die Religion*, p. 74, "It is clear that with every great historical revolution of social conditions the views and ideas of men—and with these, their religious ideas—have been revolutionized. The difference

71

this is for Marx constantly an analytic, and therefore irrefutable, proposition. For religion is the denial of the proposition that man is "the highest being for man"[12] and it is just this proposition which indicates the reality of the society of the future which the revolution is concerned to achieve. It is true that the rejection of religion, as G. Rohrmoser says in contradiction to M. Reding, is by no means "accidental" for Marx, but "implied in the concept of emancipation itself" inasmuch as the political and social liberation of man is identical with "the liberation of society from all connections with the spiritual and universal being of man, which cannot be defined in social terms".[13] But this does not amount to a definite decision about the place of the anti-religious dogma in the theory and practice of the Communist movement. And it is easy to overlook this fact, as in my opinion even Rohrmoser does. For in the unity mentioned is one which exists in the first place only for Marx himself as the unity between his theory of religion and his theory of revolution.

Now the revolution which Marx predicted and proclaimed did not occur, and (in contrast to his expectation of its nearness) is by and large not in sight. But the Communist revolution, which—with invocation of his name!—has occurred, is not the one which he expected, however much it may claim to be so. In saying this I do not wish either to bring the very complicated positive and negative relationships between Marxist thinking and the actual history of the Communist movement up to date under a primitive demagogic formula, nor do I assert that Marx and, in particular, his criticism of society have lost their actual significance for us today. The statement implies only a modest historical assertion, that the revolutionary change towards socialism in the most advanced

---

of the present revolution from all earlier ones consists precisely in this, that at last people have solved the mystery of this historical revolutionary process, that therefore and instead of vainly canonizing this practical external process under the extravagant form of a new religion, they get rid of all religion."

[12] *Frühschriften*, p. 209.   [13] Rohrmoser, op. cit. pp. 52, 61.

capitalistic industrial society prophesied by Marx, has not taken place; the revolution which did take place was the swing-over of industrially backward agrarian lands to industrialization. What in these lands is now discussed as the transition from Socialism to Communism, has only a very limited connection with the Marxist vision of the future; for it can now be said that this transition will at best fulfil some, but by no means all, of the claims which Marx made for the society of the future. We shall have to speak of that later; but this means that the problem of religion will indeed be finally "solved" for the Marxist theory concerning the future, with the conclusion of "prehistory", but that, as today every clear-sighted person can see, for the Communist movement as a real entity in the course of history, it is neither solved, nor is it going to be solved. And this, although the movement in its origins was inspired by the Marxist vision. In consequence Marxist theory will not be able permanently to avoid the necessity of reformulating its attitude to this problem, by appealing to its classical writers.

At this point two further problems in the interpretation of Marx must be mentioned. 1. It is implied in what has just been said that Marx, as his relation to Hegel will show, in fact envisages an absolute reconciliation within history of the previous contradictions of human existence—just as he proclaimed expressly as a young man: "This communism, as perfected naturalism, is also humanism, as perfected humanism, it is naturalism, it is the true elimination of the conflict of man with nature, and of man with man, the true elimination of the conflict between existence and essence, between objectification and self-activity, between freedom and necessity, between the individual and the species. It is the solution of the riddle of history, and knows itself to be this solution."[14] Although no break can be traced in Marx's life in the sense of an explicit repudiation of this vision of his youth, it can none the less be asked if it is right to see this as

[14] *Frühschriften*, p. 235.

73

the key-signature of Marx's total life-work. At least the question as to whether a more sober view later began to replace it in Marx must not be rejected out of hand. In relation to these assertions of his youth, it has often rightly been asked how after such a removal of the contradictions, history should proceed further—the same difficulty which the young Marx, together with many others, felt about the Hegelian philosophy.[15] But as his dependence on Hegel lessened, it is possible that the later Marx may have grown less confident about the absolute character of his vision of the last things. As I have said, he did not express himself on this matter— but perhaps simply because his early utterances had neither the interest for him nor for his contemporaries that they have for us as we read them today. It is therefore questionable whether we are justified in determining unhesitatingly what his concept of revolution was, by referring to his early writings. The concept remains optimistic enough if we understand it in a more relative manner, as the idea of a socialistic revolution within what is humanly possible, i.e. within the limits, and with the retention of the essential tensions, which naturally belong to man as we have known him hitherto. What is proposed then is still an utterly radical revolution, which makes great claims, something profoundly different from every kind of reformism, because its intention is, by eliminating the previous relationships of property and power, to create a condition which is radically different from the history known to us hitherto, a condition in which there is no *institutional* degradation, exploitation and compulsion of man any more, and in which all institutions are oriented towards the fostering of social feeling and a brotherly life together and for one another. Why should there not be something of this kind? Why should this be unthinkable? We should not operate too hastily with the reproach of "Utopianism", if we do not wish to expose ourselves as content, in a narrow-minded way, to put up with things as they are. In an unfortunately hitherto

[15] As in the Introduction to his Dissertation, *Frühschriften*, p. 13.

unpublished lecture on the problem of Utopia in Marx, delivered to a Conference of the Protestant-Marxism Commission, Thilo Ramm has proved that Marx's ideas about the future can very well be represented as a project for a " real Utopia"—to use a fine expression of Walter Dirks. They can thus be regarded as a rational programme, capable of discussion, whose undeniable boldness does not transgress into the realm of mere fantasy. But if this interpretation be right, Marx deceived himself in believing that the problem of religion could be eliminated by social change, and this self-deception was not rooted in his vision of the future, but is "accidental" to it, and has its roots in his limited, and—to use a favourite abusive term of his own—narrow-minded view of religion.

2. It may be asked whether the reflections of the young Marx do not contain suggestions which might have been developed in quite other directions if he had been less prejudiced against Christianity. In opposition to Hegel, understood as an idealistic philosopher of identity, Feuerbach and Marx proclaimed the stubborn independence and resistance of concrete reality to full absorption by the concept; Feuerbach championed sensation (which Hegel had neglected) over against consciousness, and Marx championed the unreconciled social reality over against the harmonizing constructions of the Hegelian doctrine of the State. Both of them were thus involved in a conflict with an idealistic pantheism similar to that which the biblical faith in the Creator has been forced from the start to wage against idealism.[16] Things were thus precisely the contrary to what they imagined them to be. They had no inkling of the traditional antithesis between

---

[16] This contradiction has been very clearly indicated by the Swedish theologian G. Aulén in *Das Christliche Gottesbild*, Gütersloh, 1930, and *Die Dogmengeschichte im Lichte der Lutherforschung*, Gütersloh, 1932.—In my opinion it is not of decisive importance whether such an interpretation was fair to Hegel's original intentions. At any rate, those younger writers, without realizing it, had the faith of the Bible on their side over against Hegel understood in this manner. I make

idealism and biblical faith since the days of the gnostics, and regarded Christianity as a mythological form of idealistic metaphysics, as indeed their Marxist successors have also done, obstinately and unteachably resistant to correction. If, instead of polemic, there had been an open conversation with biblical theology, then a representative of the latter could have pointed out to Marx a self-contradiction in his thought; misled by Hegel. Marx identified the subject-predicate re-lation—which he found in Hegel, and by means of which the concrete reality, above all, man himself, had been reduced to a mere appearance of the idea, which alone is real—with the relation between Creator and creature in Christian faith. which he now took to be the same reductive relationship. Opposing this he declared: "A being only shows itself to be independent when it stands on its own feet, and it only stands on its own feet when it owes its existence to itself. A man that lives by the grace of another regards himself as a dependent being."[17] Here, it seems, dependence on God is repudiated in the name of an absolute individualism. So Stirner also might have written. But in another place in the Paris manuscripts the tone is very different; there it is not the dignity of man to owe everything to himself alone, and to receive nothing from without; there man is seen as an objective and needy being, i.e. a being which is the object of others, and which needs others as its object, a being that stands in process of exchange. "A non-objective being is a *nonsense*." But an

---

this reply to Bockmühl's criticism (op. cit. p. 216) of my essay "Zum Verständnis des Menschen beim jungen Marx" in the *Festschrift für Günther Dehn*, Neukirchen, 1957, pp. 183–203, in which the above theme is treated at greater length.

[17] *Frühschriften,* p. 246.—A discussion of the relation between the Christian faith in creation and the Hegelian-Marxist conception of man's self-creation at this point would take too long. It may only be said, that this is by no means necessarily negative, as Marx (in the passage referred to), and many of his Christian critics think. So far as the problem dealt with is that of self-realization, what is here at stake is the right definition of the human self, man's character as subject within his relationship with God.

objective being is a being which has its nature "outside of it", which is itself "object for a third being". "It *only* creates and posits *objects, because* it is posited by objects, because it is nature from the beginning." For example, *qua* hungry, man needs "a nature beyond himself, an *object* beyond himself, in order to satisfy him, in order to quiet him". "The sun is the *object* of the plant, an object indispensable to it, which confirms its life, as the plant is object of the sun, as *expression* of the life-creating power of the sun, of the *objective* power of the sun's being."[18] The man, therefore, who, like Hegel, understands externality not as exchange, as self-expression and reception from without, and thus as a life-relationship which is to be affirmed, but rather "in the sense of a deprivation, an error, a weakness that ought not to be", such a man certainly regards true being as "something outside of himself, which he lacks" and regards nature and man as defective beings, in a manner to be distinguished from the concept of "the needy being".[19] He then regards objectivity as the equivalent of alienation, and wishes to transcend the former along with the latter. But this means that man, when his condition of defect is removed, is regarded by him as a non-objective spiritual being, without need of objects or dependence or mutuality—and this means nothing else than that "man is selfish", is "an abstract egoist". The final picture of spirit, i.e. of man in Hegel (since man is essentially spirit), is "egoism raised to its pure abstraction in thought".[20]

From this perspective it can once again be seen how far Marx regards religion as a mode of self-estrangement. If he concedes Hegel's claim to indicate the way of the divine spirit through self-emptying to self-realization, then God is here regarded as a solitary self, and if here, as Feuerbach thinks, we have to do with a human projection and, as Marx thinks, with a mystification describing the process of human consciousness, then here man is fundamentally conceived as a

---

[18] *Frühschriften*, 274, 273, 274. (Italics as in Marx.)
[19] Op. cit. p. 287.   [20] Op. cit. p. 271.

solitary self and an "abstract egoist". We do not need to question the soundness of the interpretation of Hegel here presupposed, but it does seem to me that Marx's talk about the man who relies wholly and solely upon himself, for whom every dependence and obligation to gratitude is a diminution of his independence, is a conception belonging rather to the thought-structure of "abstract egoism", which could be described by the words "Imagine a being which is neither itself an object, nor has an object! Such a being would be . . . the *only* being, there would be no being except it, it would exist in lonely solitude."[21]

Now it is true that Marx himself developed a purely this-worldly doctrine of man in relation to nature and his fellow-man. He could not have done otherwise as long as he was able to regard God as no more than a mythological expression for the reality which Hegel called "Spirit". However, in expressing his view of man's dependence on nature and his fellow-man, he did contradict his first line of argument. But if "objectivity" in relation to nature and our fellow-man is not identical with estrangement, then it is no longer *inevitable* that objectivity in relation to God, the confrontation between God and man, should be a phenomenon of estrangement. I do not claim by all this to demonstrate more than this, that the verdict about the relationship to God as a phenomenon of estrangement, as intolerable for man's self-assertion, can be logically deduced only from the first solipsistic axioms we have mentioned, but not from the position which Marx is really concerned to maintain. In the contradiction between the two lines of argument, the first anti-religious, the second anti-Hegelian, we see a conflict between a rationalistic interpretation of autonomy, and a concrete anthropology, and this justifies us in denying that it is logically necessary for Marxist anthropology to repudiate faith in God.

But then the famous statement that "Man is the highest being for man"[22] is to some extent left hanging in the air. For

[21] Op. cit. pp. 274f.   [22] Op. cit. p. 209.

where is the justification to be found for the alternative of
which it is an expression—that he who does not permit man
to be the highest being has thereby already dishonoured and
debased him, and made him a defective being that has its
nature outside of itself and not in itself? If it is no dishonour
to man compare him with a plant that owes its existence to
the sun, so also it is no dishonour to man to be lower than
God. "To be lower than God, that is the glory of the
creature."[23] If dependence is not identical with debasement.
then neither is it so in relationship to God, then neither is it
necessary for faith in man's dependence upon God, his
subordination to God, his inferior standing to God, his need
to wait upon God, to be denounced as an insult to man's
independence and greatness. Anyone who for years has read
daily that Marxist sentence inscribed on a transparency over
the gates of prisoner-of-war camps in the Soviet Union, has
had time enough to reflect upon it, and also to perceive the
contradiction between the meaning of the sentence and the
reality which he could see around him. Marx set up our
fellow-man and society as a norm for man in contradiction
to a solipsistic idealism, when he taught men to realize that
mutual dependence was an ideal which, as the treasure of
human existence, was not to be passed over in disdain. But
when at the same time he proclaimed man as "the highest
being for man", it was left open whether the highest being
for me was to be my concrete fellow-man or an idea of man in
the future. Were the first his meaning, that would lead in the
direction of the Christian love of our neighbour—with the
great difference that in the latter the claim of my neighbour
is secured by the connection between God and my neighbour,
while no man can really explain how my concrete neighbour
as such is to be the highest being for me. But if he meant the
idea of man, as Feuerbach found it in the species, and as Marx
hoped to find it realized in the society of the future, then the
concreteness which he was concerned to maintain in his

[23] K. Barth, *Church Dogmatics* III, Edinburgh 1960, p. 170.

opposition to Hegel, is only an appearance, the fellow-man who but now was so exalted, becomes without significance, and can be manipulated without redress by appealing to the idea, and the pantheism of the "solitary self" proves to be not really transcended. Or if, finally, Marx's meaning is that the highest for man should be the *relationship* between man and man—then, as in Feuerbach, the norm remains undefined which is to guide him as he lives in this relationship. In every case the result is that this saying promises more than on closer examination it is able to fulfil. Finally, however, if it is given content, as often in Engels, through the concept of man's dominion over nature, then man has the norm by which he measures his dignity, and which regulates his duties to his fellow-man, still more under his control, in his superiority over impersonal nature. It will then inevitably follow that this norm is not in a position to lay a real obligation on man, nor to confer on his fellow-man a real inviolability. When humanism deposed God in the name of humanity, it cut away the ground from under its own feet. Only when man has his norm above him will he reach his true stature. This the much-despised idealism, against which Marx had so justly protested, had nevertheless known better than he did. It was Augustine who gave the most trenchant and prophetic expression to the way in which humanism destroys itself through atheism, when he said " *Cum ergo vivit homo secundum hominem, non secundum Deum, similis est diabolo*".[24]

---

[24] Thus when man lives by man's standards, and not by God's standards, he becomes devilish. (*The City of God*, Bk. 14, chap. 4.)

CHAPTER FIVE

Messianism and Atheism

OUR previous discussion has described the type of criticism of religion which has prevailed in Marxist Communism up to the present day. No new elements have been introduced, only the changing historical situation and the tactical needs of the moment have caused changes of emphasis. In Leninism a more relaxed attitude of disregard has been replaced by "militant atheism", the commitment of the party to anti-religious agitation—as Leninism in general is Marxism in a hurry—a fact which can in part be explained by the extraneous elements of Russian revolutionary thinking which have poured into it, and in part by the secret anxiety lest the European proletariat should fail to achieve its task for humanity, and history accordingly not take the course prescribed for it by Marx. With the voluntaristic trait in Leninism, atheism also becomes militant.

But the hardening of the socialistic movement in an anti-religious mould occurred at an earlier point. The toleration within the party of church members was never regarded by Marx and Engels (who, as above noted, insisted upon it) as relativizing the fundamental conflict between socialism and religion. But to describe the views of the two spiritual fathers is not to answer the question "Why did the socialist movement adopt the anti-religious attitude?" It was in the nineteenth century that this chiefly happened, and it held good for the Communist part of the movement, while in the social-democratic part in the different European lands, the bond between socialism and atheism was to a greater or less degree dissolved.

But why not also in the Communist movement? The Labour movement was given by Marx and Engels its most important theoretical weapon. But it was not "founded" by them, both of them came from the middle classes, joined it, and became its teachers. But their teaching was never taken up holus-bolus by the whole movement, but (to the regret of the two grand old men in England!), repeatedly fused, transformed, and interspersed with elements of a different kind. Even the Marxism that Lenin adopted was not simply an orthodox restoration. The criticism of religion might conceivably not have been one of the elements adopted, and the development of a tolerance which made the relationship to religion a matter for private judgment might have influenced not only the "right wing" of the Socialist movement, but the movement itself as a whole. "What is Communism? Communism is the science which deals with the conditions of the liberation of the proletariat"—this was Engels' definition in his preliminary draft of the Communist Manifesto.[1] Thus we have here a socio-political science, and it is not immediately clear how far metaphysical theses should be an integral part of such a science. Yet even negation of faith in God is undoubtedly a metaphysical thesis. The fact that the two famous teachers of this movement gave the doctrine so universal a dimension, embracing anthropology, natural philosophy, metaphysics, time and eternity, did not compel the movement itself to take over more than its socio-political central content. Why it did not limit itself thus, why it made atheism an article of dogma, cannot be explained by referring to the authority of the two great teachers. The problem which calls for explanation is, rather, how this authority was able to impose itself so universally.

It might be possible to attribute the adoption by the

[1] *Grundsätze des Kommunismus,* 1848, MEGA VI, p. 503.

official party of the atheism of Marx and Engels[2] to the rationalist inheritance which has been of such great significance for the Labour movement. As a movement of emancipation it enters from the first on the inheritance of the Enlightenment, it is in its beginnings closely connected with the liberal bourgeoisie and its educational emancipation, and takes over the bourgeoisie's faith in reason and scientific progress, and its aversion to the clergy, dogma, and cultus. But even in the bourgeoisie that streamed to Feuerbach's lectures, the distaste for the Church's concept of God was more a climate than a dogma. This climate, together with the religious indifference of the proletariat,[3] mentioned with such satisfaction by Engels in his first work, *The Situation of the Working Classes in England*, certainly favoured the trend towards atheism, but did not actually cause it.

A further part of this inheritance is the traditional assertion that it is necessary to repudiate religion because of the avowedly irreconcilable conflict between faith and science. In the Soviet discussion today this is usually the last refuge, when people are forced to concede that the Russian Christians have broken free from the capitalist mentality, and shown

[2] The statutory expression of the dogmatic character of atheism can vary, and is conditioned by the situation. Thus it does not necessarily commit the individual party-member leaving the Church and to atheism. But this does not alter the official affirmation of atheism by the party in any way. On the essentials see Lenin's Essay "Ueber das Verhältnis der Arbeiterpartei zur Religion" (1909) in Lenin's *Ueber die Religion*, East Berlin, 1960, pp. 19ff. (pp. 26f. "Ob ein Geistlicher Miltglied der sozialdemocratischen Partei sein kann").

[3] P. 290f. "Socialism is at the same time the most decisive expression of the irreligiosity which prevails among the workers, and is so decisive in it, that the instinctively, only practically irreligious workers often shrink back at the sharpness of this expression." Similarly in an article of 1874: "Of the great mass of the German social-democratic workers one can even say that in their case atheism has already outlived itself; this purely negative word has no longer any application to them, because they stand no longer in a theoretic opposition to faith in God, but in a practical opposition to it; they have *simply done with God*, they live and think in the real world, and are therefore 'materialists' " (*Ueber die Religion*, p. 114).

their loyalty to the Soviet State:[4] no distinction is made between faith and superstition, for both are declared to be pre-scientific methods of explanation, and to hinder man from dedicating himself without blinkers or reservations to the investigation of scientific truth. Now the antediluvian theory of religion which is presupposed by these proclamations is very much more inadequate than the "inadequacy of the conceptions of religious faith" of which the Draft Programme speaks. The disputants would have to vindicate their claim to a disinterested search for scientific truth by taking into account at long last the meaning ascribed to religious statements by those who make them, and, in particular, the meaning of Christian statements about faith in God and the relationship between faith and knowledge. There are here good grounds for returning upon its authors the charge of blinkered prejudice. We must agree that in part this prejudice is due to the failure—perhaps even the continuing failure—of the Rus-

[4] Thus Stalin, addressing an American Trades Union Delegation on 9.9.1927, Works, vol. 10, Berlin, 1953, p. 116. Thus also the issue of the ZK of the Communist party of the Soviet Union of 11.11.54 (cf. *Ostprobleme* 1954/27). Lastly N. Khrushchev in his important speech at the 22nd Party Conference of the C.P.S.U. "Communist education presupposes the liberation of consciousness from religious prejudices and superstitions, which still hinder individual Soviet men from the full development of their creative powers. We need a thoroughly thought-out and harmonious system of scientific and atheist education, which will embrace all classes and groups of the population, and will hinder the spread of religious views, especially among children and young people". (*Neues Deutschland*, East Berlin, 18.10.1961). In the sketch for the new Programme of the C.P.S.U. we read: "The party uses the means of ideological education, in order to educate men in the spirit of the scientific-materialistic world-view, and to overcome religious prejudices, without allowing the feelings of believers to be injured. Patiently the inadequacy of the ideas of religious faith must be explained, ideas which arose in the past, when men lived under the pressure of blind forces of nature and in social slavery, and did not know the true causes of phenomena in nature and society. In addition we must support ourselves upon the achievements of modern science, which continually reveals more completely the picture of the world, gives man ever greater power over nature, and leaves no more place for the fantastic fables about supernatural powers." *Ostprobleme*, 1961/20, p. 647.

sian Church to draw clearly enough the boundary between faith and superstition in those areas of which the Soviets have experience. At the same time, however, Christians are increasingly proving in this area that Christian faith is no hindrance to scientific work which serves uncompromisingly the knowledge of truth, but on the contrary keeps men free from obstructive prejudicial world-views coming from other sources, which are a much greater threat.

It is equally true that the self-understanding of genuine modern science, which is itself led by the results of its work to reflection concerning the epistemological limitations immanent in its methods, and consequently denies its own capacity to produce a world-view, cannot permanently be ignored by a communist theory which continually boasts its scientific character. Here unexpected perspectives open up for a "further development of Marxist-Leninist theory" which the Programmatic Sketch describes as "the most important duty" of the party![4a]

The affirmation of science as such was not, in my opinion, from the very first, even under the intellectual conditions of the nineteenth century, the real ground for the affirmation of atheism. It would be more reasonable to see the ground in the affirmation of historical and dialectical materialism. "Science" has indeed from the first a double sense in Marxism. The positivist criterion of value (empirico-critical establishment of facts) and the Hegelian criterion (knowledge of being as a totality) are here conjoined and are indeed in conflict with one another.[5] But however Marxism may solve this problem—at any rate the atheism could be the consequence of its decision for Historical and Dialectical Materialism. Marcel Reding has denied this.[6] According to his

---

[4a] *Ostprobleme,* 1961/20, p. 646.

[5] Lenin already saw the problem, L. Kolakowski lays his finger on the wound with his contrast between critical and ideological-dogmatic Marxism, cf., his Essays *Der Mensch ohne Alternative. Von der Möglichkeit und Unmöglichkeit Marxist zu sein.* Munich, 1960, *passim.*

[6] *Der Politische Atheismus,* Graz, 1957. I do not in this study enter

argument the atheism is not—as the Marxists represent it—the logical consequence of the system of Dialectical Materialism, but on the contrary, the motive for the creation of this system. It by no means follows with logical necessity from the system, but can only be tacked on to it. Taken in itself, Dialectical Materialism is, as its representatives claim, a theory which makes generalizations, as a scientific theory should do, from the observations of the particular sciences, and gives the orientation for further work. Its special peculiarity is that for the explanation of world phenomena it admits only answers which continually take into account the connections between all these phenomena, which fit into the context of a development proceeding from inorganic material to more complicated forms, and which, to conclude, never help themselves out by the assumption of supernatural powers. Rather did they assume that the inner dynamic of this development was simply the dialectic of the self-movement of matter, which results from the dialectical character of being, i.e. from contradictions which are immanent in all existing things. Such a theory is always exposed to the question of its verification through the particular sciences, and the question of its usefulness for them, i.e. of its own value for knowledge. To exempt Dialectical Materialism from this question would be to transform it from a scientific theory into a metaphysical dogma. The decision to exclude the question of God and recourse to supernatural powers from the scientific explanation of the world does not commit one to an avowal of the atheistic position; this theory shares that decision with the whole of modern science; this is, if one may say so, the "atheism" of its method.[7] To the question concerning the relations of scientific work and Christian faith different

---

upon the discussion with Dialectical Materialism, to which today so many publications are dedicated. The statements above should make clear the legitimacy of this limitation.

[7] On the distinction between atheism as a method and atheism as a dogma, cf. my Essay, "Die Theologie im Hause der Wissenschaften" in *Ev. Th.*, 1958, pp. 28ff.

answers have emerged in the two-hundred-year-old discussion. But it is today beyond question that participation in this work, including its "atheistic method", can find a place in the life of a Christian as the work of a believer, that therefore all of us today, Christians and non-Christians, believers and atheists, find ourselves together in this work, and that consequently this work is capable of fitting in with very different general conceptions and views of the world, and does not of itself necessitate a decision for atheism. It may be that the theological formulae concerning the compatibility of science and faith do not seem personally convincing to the atheist, yet so long as he does not regard his viewpoint *par ordre di mufti* as the only possible one, he has no possibility of denying that they leave intact the rigour and freedom of scientific work, even when it is brought into a context which does not appeal to him, and whose axiomatic character he does not understand. The problems which arise within the sciences are in no way prejudiced by faith in God when this is rightly understood. Whether in physics the traditional causal formula is shaken or not, whether in biology the mathematic-causal school or the vitalistic school has the better arguments in its favour; whether in the historical disciplines the conflict between the fuller development of productivity and the traditional conditions of production is the decisive dynamic of evolution, and what part ideas and great personalities play in it, these are questions in which faith does not demand a definite party-line to be taken. Thus even the Christian can estimate without prejudice the claims of Dialectical Materialism to be a scientific theory worthy of discussion, so long as it remains what it claims to be.

Atheism—and here in my opinion we must entirely agree with Marcel Reding—does not follow from this theory, but is, on the contrary, the misuse of the "atheism of method" which prevails in it, i.e. the maxim that mundane things should be given a mundane explanation, that unknown world-phenomena should be explained in terms of known world phenomena. It changes a programme of method into an onto-logical dogma, and it does not even recognize the qualitative difference between the two. Certainly it was necessary first to learn this difference. Marxist atheism is out of date in this respect, that it remains at an intellectual stage in which there was still little clarity about the character, consequences, and limits of the methods of the natural sciences. It gave itself out at that time as the consequence of these methods, legitimating its own materialism and atheism as scientifically required by the materialism and atheism of science; it claimed that its decision was obedience to the requirements of science. In reality its decision was taken before the scientific work was done, and independently of it. By then using Dialectical Materialism to legitimate itself, it changed it from an open theory into a dogma, which from the start it does not need to be, and brings it into a confusing conflict between the claims of science and those of a world-view, with the consequence that it can really satisfy neither.

Thus we cannot accept the claim of Marxism-Leninism, that you cannot have its knowledge without accepting its world-view. Further, the fashion in which Lenin only opposes scientific theories because they still left somewhere a loophole for "fideism", a fashion which had, and still has, baneful repercussions on the scientific discussion in the Soviet Union, indicates that here the confession of a world-view, the atheistic interest, precedes the knowledge and does not flow from it. Thus our question "Where did the interest in atheism which Marx and Engels injected into the Communist movement really originate?" is still unanswered.

We should regard it as illegitimate to answer by talking about demonic powers and a "metaphysical fall", and so forth. Such a judgment lays claim to a prophetic gift of insight into the last causes of things which is not to be found at every street-corner; it tempts us to regard our opponents as devils, and makes us arrogant; we challenge the other man to repentance and at the same time avoid it ourselves; we

88

spare ourselves that trouble of looking for intelligible motives which is our first, and often enough our not easy task in our intercourse with our fellow-men.

Our question, which, as can be seen, it is by no means easy to answer, can in my opinion only be answered in a twofold manner by citing two co-operative elements of a quite diverse kind. The first is empirical knowledge, the second is Messianism.

By empirical knowledge I mean the actual things which a revolutionary social movement in the Europe of the nineteenth century was able and compelled to experience and observe in its encounter with the official representatives of Christianity—and by this I mean not only the ecclesiastical officials but also the circle of Church members taking part in religious life. These experiences, reinforced by a study of religious history, could be generalized in theoretic form. However, it must at once be noted that this element is little mentioned in Marxist theory. Empirical knowledge has only an illustrative function, and serves at the best as a subsequent confirmation of what was already known about the essence of religion.[8]

[8] Even unfavourable personal experiences are never referred to. Neither in the case of Marx nor in that of Engels, does the Biography give the key, but merely tells of the development into an irreligious thinker. As one of the sharpest expressions of Marx about the Church his article from the *Deutschen Brüsseler Zeitung* of 12.9.1847 against the article of a Consistorial Councillor may be cited (*Ueber die Religion*, p. 65). "The social principles of Christianity have now had eighteen hundred years of time to evolve, and need no further development at the hands of Prussian Consistorial Councillors. The social principles of Christianity justified ancient slavery, glorified medieval serfdom, and know equally well if necessary how to defend the oppression of the proletariat, even though with something of a pious grimace. The social principles of Christianity preach the necessity of a ruling and an oppressed class, and have for the latter only the pious wish that the former may be beneficent. The social principles of Christianity locate the compensation of all infamies, mentioned by the consistorial councillor, in heaven, and by so doing justify the continuation of these infamies on earth. The social principles of Christianity declare that all the villainies of the oppressors against the oppressed are the just punishment of original sin or of

For this reason not only the Church, but religion was the object of criticism.

But in our search for the reasons why atheism was exalted into a dogma for a whole movement we must not let ourselves be deceived by this. The development in England, where from the beginning Christian allies in the fight were visibly present, is a positive proof, as the development in Russia where the unity of State and Church made the latter a prop of the existing order is a negative proof of the fundamental importance of the historical experiences of this movement in relation to the Church Where in his wanderings could the tailor's apprentice Weitling, or the turner's apprentice Bebel, have found a manse in the Germany of that day in which a sermon would not have been preached to him on submission to his fate and humble acknowledgment of the divinely decreed order as the bearing which God required of him? From what pulpit was the collapse of the Revolution of 1848 not interpreted as a judgment of God?[9] Where was there any sign that the Church did not identify itself with the pro-

---

former sinners, or are trials which the Lord in his infinite wisdom inflicts upon the redeemed. This social principles of Christianity preach cowardice, self-contempt, abasement, servility, humility, in a word, all the characteristics of the canaille, and the proletariat, which will not let itself be treated as canaille, needs its courage, its self-respect, its pride and its sense of independence much more than even its bread. The social principles of Christianity are hypocritical, and the proletariat is revolutionary." Cf. Marx and Engels to H. Kriege, 11.5.1846.

[9] Cf. E. Schubert, *Die evangelische Predigt im Revolutionsjahr 1848,* Giessen 1913; A. Heger, *Evangelische Verkündigung und deutsches Nationalbewusstsein. Zur Geschichte der Predigt von 1806–1848,* Berlin, 1939; P. Piechowsky, *Die Kriegspredigt von 1870–71,* Leipzig, 1917. The Potsdam Court preacher, J. C. Pischon (1794), gives the generally accepted rule concerning the "use of politics in the pulpit"—it is right to encourage love and attachment to the old Constitution, to warn against our adoption of freedom and equality, to demonstrate the necessity of the differences of social station, and to give impressiveness and interest to one's words by illuminating references to the consequences of the French craze for freedom". (Quoted by H. H. Schrey, "Die Kirche und die soziale Frage" in *Theol. Rundschau,* 1953, pp. 26f.

gramme of a 'Christian State' under Friedrich Wilhem IV, and did not gratefully profit from it? Was it not evident to the thoughtful member of the proletariat that the economic order under which he suffered could not be interpreted in the categories of an idealist history? In those circles of the Church which were sensitive to the desperate urgency of the social question, were people not incapable of forming an adequate theory for its diagnosis and cure? And did not therefore all social effort remain—to use a vivid comparison of Eduard Thurneysen—like a too small lid on too large a pot?[10] Did not the urgency of material need and the object lessons taught by material work compel the proletarian to a materialistic understanding of the world, in contrast with which the idealism cherished by the Church necessarily appeared as a pale, unrealistic, misleading and deliberate confusion of the real issues? Did not theology interpret Christian faith in idealist categories, Platonic instead of Hebrew, so that it was easy to take Christianity for a special kind of idealist world-view?[11] Walter Dirks is right: "When the proletariat opened its eyes a hundred years ago and awakened to self-consciousness, it is not true that Christ was arrogantly rejected; it would be much truer to say that in a sense Christ was not there at all. Christ was invisible and inaudible. When the old Christian order of life for the peasantry and the people of the small towns was no longer viable for the proletarian, because he had been lifted out of this order into a completely different strange order, Christ should have been made visible to him in a new way through

[10] E. Thurneysen, "Sozialismus und Christentum" in *Zwischen den Zeiten*, 1923/II, p. 12f. (later reprinted in *Das Wort Gottes und die Kirche*, 1927, pp. 165–95, there at p. 170). On this point E. Thier, *Die Kirche und die soziale Frage. Von Wichern bis Fr. Naumann*, Gütersloh, 1950; H. Christ, *Christlich-religiöse Lösungsversuche der sozialen Frage im mittleren 19 Jahrhundert*. Diss. Erlangen, 1951; D. Barthels, *Die kirchenpolitischen Gruppen in ihrer Stellung zur sozialen Frage, 1870–1890*. Diss. Göttingen, 1953; K. Kupisch, *Das Jahrhundert des Sozialismus und die Kirche*, Berlin, 1958.

[11] Cf. Karl Barth on materialism as a justified corrective, *Church Dogmatics*, III, 1960, pp. 382f.

the mediation of 'Christians' who had entered into his existence in the power of Christian sacrifice. This did not happen. No Christian of stature at that point broke through the barrier between middle-class, the peasant class, and the feudal class. And so Christ remained invisible. . . . Let us be pitilessly clear on this point: this is how 'Marxism' came into existence. The Marxists fell into error, but the greater part of the blame lay with the Christians. The recognition of this fact must strike a deadly blow at the roots of all Christian self-satisfaction in relation to Marxism. The burden of proletarian unbelief lies on *our* shoulders. This unbelief does not separate us from these men, it actually binds us to them."[12]

For our inquiry we can draw hence the conclusion that, when the movement adopted the atheism of individuals as a general doctrine, its experience of the Church and its visible representatives was a decisive factor. We cannot know how things might have gone without this factor, but we can assume that the resistant power of experiences of a contrary character might have been sufficient, even in the moment of decision for the revolutionary character of the movement, to compel the drawing of a distinction between the socio-political elements and the philosophical anti-religious horizon of Marxist doctrine. But as it was, the things that men everywhere experienced at the hands of the Church, and the things that they observed in it, led straight to the adoption of this horizon, rather than refuting it.

And yet there have been exceptions which must not be

[12] "Marxismus in christlicher Sicht" in *Frankfurter Hefte*, February, 1947, pp. 141f. Cf. G. Zwerenz, "Aus dem Tagbuch eines Geflohenen" in *Der Monat*, Dec., 1959, H. 135, p. 45. "No, here you do not yet understand what Communism means. You do not see that in Communism all the anger of a disillusioned and disillusioning world blazes up. Communism—that takes its life from world-disillusionments. From longing for revenge, yes, but just as much from just anger. One cannot speak like a Christian for two thousand years, and act like a heathen. Man would not be a thinking being if that did not call forth a flood-tide. If the law of this world is really hypocrisy, then Communism is the price that has to be paid for it."

passed over in silence. From them men might have learnt to distinguish between Christianity and its empirical manifesta tions. But instead of this the fate of these exceptional figures within the Church has actually confirmed the general negative judgment. But above all it must be emphasized that our aim in what was said was not to throw stones at the graves of the fathers. It is easy to talk of "the failure of the Church in the social question" so long as, following the tradition of impenitence in the Church, even in using such language we are only concerned with the guilt of others. Certainly the attitude of the Church to social problems has altered, certainly the old prejudices have—at least to a large degree—disappeared, certainly much theoretical and practical work within the Church is dedicated to social problems. But, without wishing to underestimate the beneficial influence of individual personalities, we must say that this development is principally the consequence of the general development of the times, to which the Church is subjected both positively and negatively. The social endeavour of the Church is an expression of the trend of the times, and meets with no disapproval in society. That there is here a real victory over the old evil, an independent surge of Christian knowledge and Christian will, would have to be shown at those points which are the testing points of *today,* at which today—in another manner than in the case of the universal approved social work—an *independent* movement of the Church, which is not a consequence of the universal trend, would occur, and that not only in the form of valuable declarations of ecumenical committees, but as a movement permeating both clergy and congregation, perhaps in situations where decolonialisation goes against white interests (Katanga, Nyasaland, Rhodesia, Algeria, Angola), or in the question of mass weapons of destruction. So long as people in the Church assert that they regard these as a useful means of defence against the "Bolshevist murder of the soul", that they regard the privileges secured in the western lands to the Church—at least its legal establishment by the State which obtains here—as an indispensable presupposition for the existence of the Church—so long then as people—quite against the New Testament (cf. Matthew 10)—think that Christian existence is only possible behind a protective political wall and under special social conditions, so long will they confirm the Communists in their view of the class-character of religion and confirm them in their error. These words quoted above from Walter Dirks would have to be descriptive of the general knowledge and attitude of Christians, if the complaint of J. L. Hromadka that the attitude of the Church today, "especially in its crusade against the East and Communism", confirms and makes credible "with a depressing accuracy the Marxist philosophy of religion",[13] is to be made redundant. New empirical knowledge creates a new situation, even for Communism. Therefore from the deductive character of the Marxist criticism of religion, and from its failure to mention the empirical factor, we must not draw the conclusion that the latter has no decisive significance. In my opinion it has *the* decisive significance—not so much for Marx himself, as for the adoption of his repudiation of all religion as party doctrine.

In passing, without entering upon the individual questions which are grouped around this point, I may at least mention that one of the most difficult problems which, in addition to historical inadequacies and rigidities, from the beginning alienated Marxism from the Church, was the problem of revolution. Marxism at once aligned itself with that tradition in Socialism which advocated violent revolution as an inevitable transitional phase. But the attitude of the Church to revolution was hostile from the beginning. And even without the special form of the Lutheran doctrine of authority and the conservative opposition of the Church in the nineteenth century to the slogan of the sovereignty of the people, a revolutionary labour movement inevitably came into conflict

[13] In "Antwort" (*Festschrift zu Karl Barths 70 Geburtstag*), Zürich, 1956, p. 1.

94

not only with the empirical Church, but also with the ethic of the Church, which in its interpretation of the divine commandment admitted only the legitimacy of striving for reforms which could be peacefully achieved, but not the preparation for violent revolt. We must here confine ourselves to mentioning the problem, in which ethics and historical experience are especially closely intertwined, in such a manner that, as contemporary discussion about the right of resistance shows, it is necessarily an open question, and not one which is to be decided once and for all by the application of timeless decrees. The Church's warning against revolution may well contain a sober truth in face of a too-hasty recourse to violence, in face of the belief in violence so deeply rooted in the Communist movement, in face of every revolutionary mystique, and especially in face of what I shall later call the "Religion of Revolution". But the belief that the phenomenon of modern revolution could be understood by means of the traditional categories of revolt and the murder of tyrants, was indequate. So in this matter both sides had, and have, to learn from each other. But in the nineteenth-century situation of historical knowledge, Marxism, faced through the Church's veto on revolution by the alternative of choosing between its conviction of the necessity of revolution and the command of God which forbids revolution, decided for revolution and against a God who seemed by his veto merely to sanction the existing order.

And yet it would be wrong to see the empirical factor as the only one. It was necesary that there should be another, which involved a decision which is certainly "irrational", without thereby being regarded as demonic. It was the decision to give Communism as "the doctrine of the conditions of the liberation of the proletariat" such an expansion that the struggle received over and above its socio-political goal an eschatological Messianic character, or, more precisely, it was the decision to adopt the expansion which this doctrine had received at the hands of Marx and Engels. This expansion was indeed traditional among the early socialists, who also were unable to paint the necessary social revolution in any other than the eschatological colours of paradise. This meant that the labour movement was already receptive for the Marxist perspective. How far this absolute perspective should be obligatory on the movement, how far it must and should give up its right as the firstborn to its task in world-history, for the mess of pottage of particular improvements, this has in consequence been a problem causing division within the labour movement, which gave rise to the opposition between reformism and revolution, between trade-unionism and Leninism, and which is a latent factor in the conflicts between the factions of Communism today; the Messianic exaggeration begets ever again the temptation of a merely pragmatic way of thinking, and a limitation to the tasks of the day.

And with all this it is impossible to decide the question which reaches into the unfathomable depths of the human heart, whether the absolute character of the chosen goal is the result of the repudiation of religion, or on the contrary, has caused it. The rejection of faith in God may be the consequence of a defiant and triumphant emancipatory self-assertion of man. But this self-assertion can also have the function of positively filling the vacuum[14] which came into existence through the preceding disillusionment with the Church and the disintegration of religion. Both factors may in the history of modern thought have indistinguishably influenced each other as cause and effect; the claim of God was doomed to rejection because it was understood as hindering and competing with the claim of man to self-development, which—whatever its grounds may have been—was asserting itself with great force. On the other hand man needed a new prospect of earthly self-development as a substitute and consolation for the loss of the faith which had been destroyed

[14] Cf., for example, Ignazio Silone in his contribution to *Der Gott, der keiner war*, 1952, p. 91. "Who can picture the secret dismay, which the final renunciation of the faith in immortality calls forth?" Cf. also the later publications of Arthur Koestler.

by the Enlightenment, and for the loss of the rich sense of significance which is given by faith. Thus absolute Communism needs atheism, but equally atheism, in so far as it is not able to tolerate resignation, needs earthly promises of so absolute a character as those Communism provides. Thus the Marxist formulae, too, can quite well be reversed; when man loses heaven (perhaps through the discovery that it is empty) how else shall he console himself than with the earth, and in what other way than by cheating himself with the illusion that the earth is capable of producing a compensatory consolation, and that only the hitherto imperfect conditions are to blame for the fact that men had not hitherto believed that it was able to provide such consolation? The liberation of the proletariat must at the same time be the liberation of man in general, the introduction of the absolute society, in which the interests of the individual and the interests of the species, coincide, in which the riddle of history is solved, in which, as George Lukacs often wrote, it becomes evident that however tragic the fate of the individual existence may be, the lot of man as a whole is not tragic; in which man's wishes which go beyond his earthly life are a thing of the past, have "died out" because he finds in fellowship the fulfilment of all his genuine needs.[15] By fighting for itself, the proletariat becomes

[15] As an example the graphic formulation of the vision of the future by the French Marxist, H. Lefebre (since liquidated in a party crisis). From H. Lefebre—N. Gutterman, *Introduction à Lenine,* quoted by J. Lacroix and H. de Lubac, *Der Mensch in marxistischer und Christlicher Sicht,* Offenburg, 1948, pp. 69f. "The total man will be real, as these words (of the young Marx) express it. . . . The human element, both inwardly and outwardly, goes right down to the foundations of nature, and appropriates nature most intimately as a god, and it is most profoundly transcended in the human, and lifted up to the level of spirit. The unity of the individual and the social, the possession of nature, including his own nature, by man—that is what the total man signifies. . . . He is truly one who is 'all', he possesses, he conceives, he forms his well-being from out of the whole of nature. . . . Human completeness hitherto remained dissipated and full of contradiction. It waited for its unity, that means, for the true man, for the realization of its being." (On this read E. Bloch!)

the fulcrum for the great, universal change; but for this reason it must never fight for itself alone, "its Fatherland must be greater".

1. The plan of battle for this battle—this is the first point at which is shown the logical necessity of atheism for this communism that affirms this Messianic perspective—must be materialistic and must place materialism under an atheistic sign. For the *absolute* goal is displayed not merely as a consolatory hope, but at the same time as a motive for action. If it is to be the goal of a human action, then the thought of a divine gift must be excluded. Only for an absolute goal, and only when this goal is given into his hand alone, will man exert himself absolutely. The thought of God might lead to lack of self-assurance and to indolence. Atheism leads to adjustment, to closing of the ranks, to the disciplining of a fighting force with a Messianic absolute goal; it is an ingredient of the Communist revolution in its Messianic phase.

2. The struggle is meaningful only if the goal within earthly history is *attainable*, if those manifestations from which, according to religious belief, only supernatural help can redeem us, can be removed by self-redemption and immanent evolution. This is the real motive for opposition to faith in the Creator; the doctrine of *generatio aequivoca*, of man's self-creation through work, has not only the aim of excluding the divine Creator as answer to the causal question concerning the origin of man,[16] its real goal is purposive, man in the past must have come into being by creating himself because the new man, the man of the future, can only come into existence by creating himself.

3. The activity of man himself directed to such a goal presupposes that man can dominate history, and this again pre-

---

[16] *Frühschriften*, p. 246. "The theory of *generatio aequivoca* is the only practical refutation of the theory of Creation", then developed by Engels in his essay on "The Part played by Work in the Humanization of the Ape". However, even Old Testament scholarship today studies the biblical accounts of Creation in their eschatological aspect. Cf. L. Köhler, *Theologie des Alten Testaments*, 1935, p. 71.

supposes that nature and history, and in particular their laws, can be exhaustively known. Religion regards realms of being as in principle unsearchable, and by so doing impedes the disinterestedness, intensity, and confidence of research. Therefore that group whose activity is the revolution directed to an absolute goal, and which needs for this a relentless will to knowledge, must break with religion as an enemy of knowledge, and proclaim that in the last resort the world and life are without mystery.

4. In particular this holds good for the knowledge of society. Man must perceive that the powers which dominate the life of society, and at first glance appear anonymous, are really his own productions, and therefore can be dissolved, as they were created, by him. But the traditionalism and conservatism peculiar to religion result in its investing these anonymous powers and orders (ranging from Government, the difference between poor and rich, to wars and crises) with the aura of divine decree, and encourages man to react to them with submission rather than with rebellion. "This consolidation of our own product to a material power over us, which grows beyond our control, thwarts our expectations and makes vain our calculations",[17] drives ignorant men to hypostatize their dependence in a religious manner, and thereby gives support to the dominance of these powers. (Here, moreover, Schleiermacher's concept of religion—the feeling of absolute dependence—may have played its part.) The revolutionary group must, on the contrary, realize that man is, and creates, his own fate. By so doing it snatches at the same time from the ruling class one of the most important instruments for keeping down the oppressed. The revolution needs criticism of ideologies, the ruling group needs ideological rigidities. Therefore the conception of powers subject neither to change

[17] K. Marx, *Die deutsche Ideologie*, p. 30; *Das Kapital*, vol. I, p. 585: "As in religion man is dominated by the shoddy product of his own head, so in capitalist production he is dominated by the shoddy product of his own hand." Cf. Lenin, *Ueber die Religion*, pp. 23f.

nor influence, freely and mysteriously dominating man, must be given up, in political economy as in theology, and so long as it is not given up in theology, i.e. so long as every kind of theology is not given up, the conception is not really given up in political economy either.

5. The revolutionary group must bind every one of its members and, beyond this, every man whom it can reach, exclusively to this goal, i.e. it must proclaim to all the attainable goal of a perfect condition of humanity as a task and a promise, which alone can give a true and absolutely adequate meaning to the existence of every individual. This signifies that the meaning of human existence lies wholly in the earthly human fellowship, and that no other meaning is possible. If man can cast a longing glance at another meaning, he will not dedicate himself wholly to the work for this earthly fellowship, he will also console himself too quickly about its defects instead of resolutely removing them. By making earthly things penultimate, religion takes away their seriousness and importance. By setting a heavenly goal and by substituting the transcendent God-man dialogue for the I-Thou dialogue within the world, it individualizes, fixes the interest of man in his private destiny, and promises him a private fulfilment independent of the fulfilment of humanity and in abstraction from it: man has no longer an absolute need of his fellow-man, and since instead of the human fellowship God becomes for him the highest, his own salvation really becomes the highest for him: religion is egoism.[18] Therefore the revolutionary group must break with religion and work against its influence.

6. In order to strive for the goal of a this-worldly perfection with all his powers, a member of the revolutionary group must not only be inescapably bounded by this world; he must also proclaim that he welcomes this limitation. No thought

[18] Thus Marx had already read in Holbach (cf. *Die Heilige Familie*, p. 264): "Ethics proves to him, that of all beings the most necessary to man, is man. . . . Every ethic which separates our interests from those of our fellow-men, is false, insensate, against nature. . . . The religious ethic never serves to make mortals more sociable."

must be permissible which might lure him beyond these limits. What belongs to this world is characterized by concreteness and material character. Everything non-concrete and non-material must therefore be represented as secondary; spirit as a late product of matter, consciousness as a product of the brain, the ideas as reflections of the relations of production, religious ideas as phantasmagoria, religion and metaphysics as twin-brothers, both of which sacrifice reality for a dream.[19] Attempts of theologians to distance themselves from idealism are not accepted, since at all events a transmundane reality is posited with the concept of God, which relativizes the reality of this world;[20] while the revolutionary group needs a concept of reality which epistemologically and ontologically is secured against every kind of transcendence. "The world is self-sufficient"[21]—this must be the central axiom of the whole doctrine.

And so this wordly eschatology with its Messianism is the internal ground of the dogmatic affirmation of atheism, as the empirical knowledge of the Church was its external ground. The fighter in a revolution with a goal of this kind cannot get on without a revolutionary metaphysic, without a general picture of the world, without a "world-view". The goal, seen in the vision, seized by the will, requires a world-picture which justifies it in thought. The break-away from religion happens just at this point; Marxism becomes a substitute-religion by becoming a substitute source of meaning.[22] From this standpoint it is understandable how well-founded

[19] Marx: Christianity is "the perfected philosophy of transcendence" (MEGA I, 1, i, p. 13).
[20] E.g. Klaus, *Jesuiten, Gott, Materie,* p. 134. "The Thomistic reality does indeed exist outside human consciousness . . . but it does not exist outside every kind of consciousness, e.g., not outside of the consciousness of God, and so Thomistic Realism is nothing other than objective Idealism."
[21] Ibid. p. 318; E. Bloch, *Das Prinzip Hoffnung,* III, p. 298.
[22] See the quotation from J. R. Bloch, p. 11, Note 1; H. J. Lieber, "Marxistisches Sendungsbewusstsein. Der Heilsanspruch des Marxismus" in *Deutsche Universitätszeitung,* 1956/2, and 3.

individual objections of a historical, logical, politico-economic nature often cut no ice in discussion with our Communist partners. This world-view was not in fact conceived to satisfy the theoretic questions of a mind in repose. No, it is a fighting doctrine, and therefore satisfies so long as the objective of the battle is believed in, and the loyalty of the fighting-group is intact. If reality contradicts the doctrine—then, in good Hegelian fashion—so much the worse for reality! The fighter wills that the world should be as it is here conceived, because he can then realize his goal. Or: because the world is as it is, there is therefore nowhere a goal and meaning for man except in this perspective of the attainable absolute society within history. The deepest roots of this atheism are thus—contrary to the official claims—not theoretic, not "scientific", but practical. Atheism is the postulate; God cannot exist because his existence would exclude self-redemption. But this postulate can, as already stated, have grown from the deeper soil of the experience of meaninglessness after the disintegration and loss of faith in God; it cried out to be transcended in the discovery of a new meaning. This has happened here, and the confident tone expresses the conviction that the crisis which originated with the question about the meaning of existence without God, has been successfully surmounted. All theoretic argumentation *pro et contra* conceals the existential ground of the decisions; it can only confirm these after the event, give weapons for the fight. But the decisions are taken at a deeper level. This means, however, that the man who makes the decisions, and who is to be led beyond a previous decision, must be sought for at a deeper level than that at which he would at first like to carry on the discussion.

Atheism as the obligatory doctrine of a revolutionary movement is then once and for all bound up with the fate of an absolute eschatology of immanence. And this itself is once and for all bound up with the progress and fate of the movement and its struggle. However absolutely it may be formulated as allegedly timeless truth, it belongs all the same to the historically-conditioned ideology of the movement, conditioned by the mental, social, and political climate of the time of its origin, by the development of the relation between faith and science, by its experiences from time to time in relation to religious groups, and last but not least by the difference of the situation before and after it seizes political power, i.e. by its failure to realize its programme. The doctrine does not continue permanently unchanged through the changes of experience and situation. And here we must note that a movement, so long as it is still looking forward to the seizure of power, can turn a blinder eye in its doctrine to the influence of historical process than later; its adherence to its Utopia is less likely to be disputed. After the seizure of power it is in the saddle, the conservative tendency of possession, the desire to keep things as they are, influences it, and at the same time the responsibility for a concrete society for men, for their existence and needs, is not permanently to be ignored. Further, there is the testing-out of projects in their execution, there are the reverses, the unforeseen new factors, the differences of opinion which now begin to show even in the ranks of the rulers, the different national conditioning factors, and so on, and the eventually resulting loss of the monolithic character of the movement, which was so much easier to maintain in the days of struggle. Finally, there is the great problem, intractable to the direction of even very strong leaders, of handing over to the next generations, a problem which repeatedly causes the older generation to experience the limits of its own power and influence.

At a distance from reality goals are often formulated as absolute Utopias (so once was even the liberal Utopia, whose fruits even the conservatives of the West today would never wish to renounce!). But on a nearer prospect expectations become more sober. The attainable is separated from the unattainable. The Utopian absolute formulation had its historical function as a stimulant, but it cannot be turned into the prose of reality.

103

The Exaggerated Demands made on Utopia by Messianism

THE last sentences might give the impression that Christian critics would sit by rubbing their hands in the certainty that earthly things appear much more prosaic in reality than they do in imagination, and that I am recommending that the cause of faith should be furthered by scepticism. Frequently on the Christian side it is argued against Marxism that the world and man cannot be improved. We shall later have to remark how much justice there is in this claim. But in the first place this sceptical tone produces an unfortunate impression. It has been the constant practice of unimaginative conservatism to denounce as an unreal Utopia whatever went beyond the limits of previous experience, and yet we owe indispensable achievements of progress to those who did not respect the limits of what appeared possible at the time. And can this picture be satisfying to Christians: the atheist as advocate of a great hope for humanity, and on the other side the Christian as an advocate of scepticism, and scepticism as a protective wall for Christianity? *Spiritus sanctus non est scepticus. . .* The Holy Spirit is not a sceptic [Luther against Erasmus]— should this word of Luther not warn us against such an allocation of positions? Can we leave out of account the fact that the Christian hope is the ground in which even this atheistic eschatology is rooted? Can the contradiction consist in this, that the Christians in the name of a transcendent hope should abandon the world to its incorrigibility and its misery, and that in answer to this the Marxists should with August Bebel leave heaven to the angels and the sparrows? That would surely rather be the antithesis between Platonism and Marxism than that between Christianity and Marxism, and precisely for this reason could imply a warning against the Platonizing of Christianity.

Nietzsche's call "Brothers, to the earth be true!" then contradicts rather a Christian Platonism than Christian faith itself, which is precisely a new hope for this earthly world, and indeed, not a smaller and paler faith than that which Marxism proclaims, but a greater one. The fact that Marxism as a descendent brings only a substitute for this hope, that it originated from the paralysing of this hope, and consequently as a result of resignation, has the consequence that, as we have yet to show, it contains a resignation. Much more radical and all-embracing is the Christian hope. It originates through the reception of the promise that the Creation shall really come to its goal, that everything which frustrates it shall be overcome and thrust aside, including evil, but even more, death—still more, death in us, wickedness, sin in its deepest roots. True, this hope is not directed to a future earthly paradise, but to "a new heaven and a new earth", i.e. to a fulfilment which transcends the categories of this world, and whose centre is a new relationship between man and God. And certainly this hope is not based on confidence in the success of human action, but on the faithfulness of him who gave the promise and does not deceive us with it. But none the less this hope embraces the earth and nature and bodily existence, and does not make human action meaningless; it alone gives it meaning.[1] It is not primarily on sceptical

[1] W. Kreck, *Die Zukunft des Gekommenen*, Munich, 1961, p. 165: "Here is made clear whether the Gospel of Jesus Christ is a reality, the power which concerns my life here on earth, in this body, in which I live, in which I sin, in which I have fellowship with others, in which also I suffer death, or whether it is only a theory, something within me, or belonging to another world." "A faith which leaves the future empty, which speaks of it only in negative terms, or merely of a futurity of God, is in a certain danger of also leaving ethics without content, i.e. at least only giving us negative warnings that action on earth can never anticipate the last things, but for the rest leaving earthly life to itself. But a faith which in reality reckons with the fact that the life of Jesus Christ should 'be glorified in our mortal body', can only see this earthly bodily life in the light of this

grounds, but because of this greater hope, that Christian criticism of Marxist Messianism becomes inevitable. The hope of Christian faith mobilizes on the one hand the Christian to make visible on earth signs of the Kingdom of God, through active protest against misery, against the sloth and lack of imagination of reactionary stubbornness, and places him on the side of the revolutionary, unites him with the latter's revolt against the existing order, and makes it possible from time to time for a whole series of steps to be taken in common. But just this hope, in its radical character and scope, which is based on God's promise, makes one also sober with respect to the possibilities in the world. More than signs, than small, inadequate movements towards the Kingdom of God they cannot and should not be, they cannot remove the burden of the earth, they cannot eliminate its actual incorrigibility. To this extent scepticism is actually inherent in the Christian faith. From this there results the conservative trend in Church history, which must be resisted through the reflection on the legitimate place of scepticism *within* the Christian hope.

The Alterable and the Unalterable

It is not so important to criticize the Utopian element in a critical manner, as to point out the contradiction between the limitations of Utopia and the claims it makes.

---

coming life—and without wishing to anticipate this coming life—must be determined that our ethical action should be a witness to the life to come. The man who, like Paul, expects from the future, that the last enemy, death, shall be destroyed—that, however inconceivable this may be for us—'this corruptible will put on incorruption, and this mortal immortality' . . . sees in the light of the promise of this future the whole of earthly life already in the grasp of this coming reality of God, and cannot therefore reconcile himself so easily to the laws of death of this world" (ibid. p. 175). Cf. also E. Thurneysen, "Christus und seine Zukunft" in *Zwischen den Zeiten*, 1931, vol. 3, and H. D. Wendland, "Christliche und Kommunistische Hoffnung" in *Marxismusstudien*, 1953, 1st Series (reprinted in *Botschaft an die soziale Welt*, Hamburg, 1959, pp. 177–201.

Utopianism has in it a hidden element of resignation, which betrays itself in its limitation, and it is precisely this which is the target of Christian criticism. Faith and atheism must test themselves by reality when they struggle with one another.[2] The so confident critics in the nineteenth century were not aware that the religious promise looks at those boundaries at which the promise of the critics must fail, at which labour, progress, fellowship, etc., can no longer be sources of meaning. What happens when incurable disease, deformity, age condemn one to an inactive life useless to the community? What of the power of the instincts, the fire of jealousy, and the poison of inferiority complexes, the unequal distribution of gifts and the resultant inequality of opportunity? Will they press less heavily on socialized man—or perhaps more heavily? What of the burden of guilt and the problem of the unburdening of conscience, and the problem of forgiveness? How about death? Feuerbach is continually touching on these questions, but his discussions of them are so superficial, that they must rather be regarded as attempts to evade them. Hans Ehrenberg was right to call him "A man who did not know death and misunderstood evil".[3] But the case is no better when we read, for example, in a Soviet party newspaper, "The presence of a residue of religion is to a certain degree connected with the fact that man has not yet become completely master of nature. In spite of the colossal successes of science and technics men have not yet fully liberated themselves from such destructive forces of nature as drought, flood, and other natural catastrophes."[4]

The selection, by means of which the burden of nature is confined to cases of catastrophe, is revealing. Friedrich Engels, in the words of his *Anti-Dühring* (p. 38, note 46),

[2] So rightly H. H. Schrey, "Der politische Atheismus" in *Libertas Christiana, Festschrift für Fr. Delekat*, Munich, 1957, pp. 159–74.
[3] In his edition of Feuerbach, *Philosophie der Zukunft*, 1922, p. 94.
[4] *Partinaja Shisni*, Moscow, 1958, No. 24, quoted in *Ostprobleme*, 1959/1, p. 26.

quoted above, has given unconsciously and without reflection the criterion by which to measure whether in the offer of a completely valid substitute for the Christian faith, there was present an adequate awareness of what was really at stake. He spoke of the "last power" which must be abolished; he said when "nothing more" made man dependent, then religion would die out, and we referred at that early point to the way in which his words echoed the Pauline statements in the Resurrection chapter of the First Letter to the Corinthians. If we take Engels at his word, then it soon becomes clear that he was only thinking of social dependence and dependence on nature, but of both only in an at once restricted measure. What is happening here? Either in a surreptitious self-deception what is alterable is depicted as the whole, in order not to endanger the illusion of the attainability of the condition of absolute harmony—or in a kind of pedagogic deception what is alterable is placed in the foreground, and everything else is trivialized and glossed over, in order to concentrate man's energies on what is alterable, in the belief that only the energies directed to this goal will be meaningfully invested, whereas the effect of looking at the unalterable will have the result that even what is alterable will not be altered.[5] If the

[5] Cf. Bert Brecht's posthumous poem, "Keinen Gedanken verschwendet an das Unänderbare," 1930, published in *Sinn und Form*, East Berlin, 1960/3, which begins with the words: "Waste no thought on/ What cannot be altered/ Take no hold of/ What cannot be bettered . . ." and ends: "As good technicians wish to drive at the end at its highest speed/ The car built with so much trouble and with so many improvements/ That it may show everything that it's got, and the farmer wishes/ To plough the field with his perfected plough, and as the bridgebuilders/ Long to let loose the giant dredger on the gravel of the riverbed/ So we wish to go forth and bring to an end the work of improving/ This planet for the whole of living humanity." Then later Marx expressed similar views in his famous words about the kingdom of necessity and of freedom (*Das Kapital*, vol. 3, pp. 873f.) only more with a view to a contraction of the former and an expansion of the latter, and thus of a relative shifting of the boundary. Therefore E. Thier, "Ueber den Klassenbegriff bei Marx" in *Marxismusstudien*, 3rd Series, pp. 183, 177), says,

latter was his intention, then it is clear that his claim to destroy religion becomes entirely without foundation, and then also the expectation that it will die out in the socialist society has no justification.

In any case, the man who undertakes to compete with the Christian message must face up without quibbling to the hard realities of irremediable inequality, of guilt and death. Feuerbach could only counsel men to understand death as the "revelation of love" because it was the negation of independent existence, to believe in "the imperishable youth of humanity",[6] to strengthen by means of death the "consciousness of the species",[7] and to "replace the world beyond our grave in heaven by the world beyond our grave on earth, the historical future, the future of humanity".[8] Marx—probably also remembering words of Hegel[9]—called death "the hard victory of the species over the individual",[10] and in the preparatory work for his Dissertation found that the idea of an individual immortality had "an unspeakable aridity" and was, with its intention of "remaining in singularity" both unreasonable and immoral, appealing to Jakob Böhme:

"Who counts but one, time and eternity—
That man is from all striving free."[11]

---

rightly, that in Marx the contradiction remains "unsolved" between the eschatology compelled within this-worldly limits and a "realism" with regard to the problems remaining even in the classless society (thus "the effectual continuity of earthly things, in spite of the revolutionary change").

[6] *S.W.*, vol. 3, pp. 17f., 82.

[7] "Das Wesen des Christentums", pp. 236f.

[8] "Vorlesungen über das Wesen der Religion" in *S.W.*, vol. 8, p. 364.

[9] E.g. *Phänomenologie*, Jubilee Edition, vol. 2, p. 344; *Philosophie der Religion*, vol. 15, p. 192; *System der Philosophie*, Part I, vol. 8, p. 433: "The living thing dies, because it is the contradiction, *in* itself to be the universal, the species, and yet immediately only to exist as the individual. In death the species shows itself as the power over the immediate individual."

[10] *Frühschriften*, p. 239.

[11] MEGA I, 3, pp. 111–15. On the problem of death see also E.

In his later years, to my knowledge, he avoided all mention of the problem of death.

Individual and Society

It can hardly, however, escape notice that such words merely palliate and gloss over the dread boundary of annihilation, and the manner in which death brings home to the individual the fact that his life is being called in question. With the three realities mentioned there show themselves the factors which above all give individual character to human existence, which force man back to ask the question of his own being. In these experiences the identification of the individual with society reaches its boundary, they continually call this identification in question, and through them unanswerable questions are put. And while society can for a time console us for this failure, our life in society cannot answer them. They prevent the complete submersion of the individual in society. The personal relations between individual people do not correspond with those between the individual and society; from them we learn that every man stands in a number of relationships, none of which can replace the others, and which can come into tragic conflict with one another. This ensures that the overcoming of these conflicts, however large a part custom, taboo and material compulsion may play, is also always a *moral* happening, not merely a biologically necessary process, as in the case of the ant or the termite, but a happening in which man as an individual participates in his freedom. Were the individualization of which we speak to "die out", then men would no longer experience personal individual love as a most intimate and exclusive dialogue, they would no longer

Bloch, *Das Prinzip Hoffnung*, II, p. 63, III, pp. 270f. One should compare, how poets recognize death as *the* unsolved problem for conditions of society, which have left far behind them the Marxist problems of alienation of "prehistory"; A. Huxley in *Brave New World*, and F. Werfel in *Der Stern der Ungeborenen*.

meet death and guilt as the experiences that separate them out and individualize each one, experiences in which they are compelled to say "I", and in which no one else can represent them. It is precisely to this reality so rich in conflict that the Christian message speaks, while the Marxist message has no word to say to it. For it regards these conflicts and these separations, and consequently the tension between the individual and society, as a regrettable defect which ought to be overcome. With the removal of the disturbance of society through these conflicts, that reality would have died out which the religious question always involved, and to which the Christian faith gives an answer. But with it there would have perished also the richness, the positive tension of human existence in general.[12]

The Question of Meaning

In these reflections we have so far taken Marxism at its word as to opt for an absolute understanding of its promise. We are justified in so doing by the standard that it has set for itself with its claim to replace all religion, and with it also the Christian faith. We shall later have to remind ourselves that, as we have just indicated, a more modest interpretation is also possible. But first that standard must be more widely applied; and this we shall do by considering the question of meaning, and press on to deal with the factors of inequality, guilt, and death, which disturb reflection on this question. It is, of necessity, formulated and answered in Marxist thought in just as much reduced terms as we saw before used in the question of death. The question of meaning gets its greatest urgency when it becomes the question of the meaning of the

[12] M. Reding therefore once gave in a lecture food for deep thought as to what else would also have to "die out" as a presupposition for the "dying out of religion", and what other things would all die out at the same time as religion!

individual human life. The man who answers it with a reference to the function of the individual life in relation to the species, contradicts by so doing his claim to be a humanistic thinker, for he has given an answer equally valid—or more so —in the case of the brutes, an answer in the light of which the specific problems of humanity can only be regarded as pathological symptoms. The fact that a man can regard such a reference as an answer, and further, an adequate answer, implies that fundamental decisions have been taken in one's thinking concerning man and concerning the attainment of human reality. In Christian thought (and not in religious thought in general—here the failure to make a distinction between the gospel and the religions takes its revenge!) an unprecedented, supreme accent is laid, as Marx suspected, but wrongly expressed it, on the individual life, and not only through "insistence on individuality", but because the content of the gospel is the victory of the love of God. This love is directed to every man, and further, to the individual man. It does not isolate him, but it individualizes him in the same way as the love of the father and mother does with each individual child, however large the number of children. This means: 1. For this love every single person is irreplaceable. 2. Every individual is immediately related to God and therefore is not submerged in indifference either in respect of his life or in respect of his individual acts—but neither can he hope to become a matter of indifference, hiding himself in or behind the crowd in which the individual counts for nothing. 3. Every individual is more than the species. He lives in the collective, and not without the collective,[13] but he neither lives for the collective alone, nor from the collective alone, but as one loved by God in a relation which embraces the relation

[13] N. Khrushchev at the 21st Party Conference of the Communist Party of the Soviet Union, January 1959, with loud applause: "Man is a social being, whose life outside the collective is not thinkable" (*Die Welt*, Hamburg, of 29 Jan., 1959).

to the collective, but does not coincide with it; he lives from and for God, and this means that he finds his meaning in a personal relationship which far transcends his earthly function in society, above the categories of social profit and social adaptation—though admittedly it is by no means indifferent to the latter. 4. He has now, and already in his relation to God's love his meaning and security, he does not have to wait until some future conditions are fulfilled, he has it unconditionally and without possibility of loss. This is what the New Testament means by its word, "Nothing can separate us from the love of God". (Rom. 8:39.)

If this relation to God, in which the proclamation of the gospel places us, is denied, then necessarily the consequence follows that the individual is regarded as a matter of indifference, or at least there results an embarrassment which cannot be permanently concealed by various attempts to answer the question where the significance of the individual is to be found. Yet this is a question whose answer is of the utmost importance for the evaluation of the individual's life, for our intercourse with him, and for the moral claims we make on the individual. Man is now alone in a world where it is very easy to replace him, in which he has only a fleeting and soon-forgotten place, a world as little capable of giving him enduring value as it is of receiving it from him. Thus he lives within an ultimate horizon of indifference. Within this horizon, however, the world as a totality also stands, since it too only moves in itself and revolves around itself,[14] and has no significance for any counterpart—an enlarged edition of the same "abstract egoist" which Marx saw and repudiated in the Hegelian concept of Spirit. All phenomena within it are the

---

[14] The old thought of the Eternal Recurrence, taken up again by Engels (Introduction to his *Dialektik der Natur*, East Berlin, 1952, pp. 18f.). It is, however, not brought into harmony with his teleology of progress. The meaninglessness of this first concept, the later Nietzsche, in contrast with the cheerful insouciance of Engels, realized with horror.

victims of time; so they cannot be the source of any enduring significance. Thus in his search for significance man can only turn to man. But our individual fellow-man, just as transitory and just as imperfect, cannot bear this burden—however much in practice in the individual case a man may attach himself to a neighbour as a source of hope and meaning. In appearance, humanity as a whole, which, as we learnt from Feuerbach, so long survives the individual, is better equipped for this role. But it is a highly abstract entity, and it is necessary to shut one's eyes to the fact that it, too, is a transitory phenomenon in the cosmos.[15] Meaning presupposes a permanent court of appeal. Since in this case there is none, there is placed on the shoulders of man and humanity a burden which they are not able to bear, and a task they are not able to fulfil. So even here in the last resort man must cease to be a recipient and become himself the source of action; the problem of meaning acquires an activistic significance; there is no meaning, but I give one, by deciding to find the meaning of my life in pledge for the progress of humanity, or, to put it more clearly, to pretend that I do so. "There is" no other meaning than that which I myself attach to the world, to life, to my life. Thus, however, this position—which is of course in the post-Christian age not confined to Marxism, but is shared by it—is disclosed as an intensely subjectivist one, and must necessarily be so, since the modern science which is here cited as the final court of appeal, remains silent on the question of meaning. This subjectivism—and it is pre-

[15] Engels touches on this nihilist perspective, when, in his *Dialektik der Natur* (p. 28) he conjectures, that even life on the earth, which now—according to his optimistic conviction—is moving on the rising gradient of its development, will one day have died out. He brushes this off with the nonchalant remark that "everything that comes to be deserves its own calamity", but obviously does not remember that this word was of set purpose put in the mouth of Mephistopheles, and he closes with the consoling thought that nature could create the same masterpiece on another star, and that thus the extinction of life on the earth does not mean a universal end of life in the Cosmos.

cisely at this point that Heidegger's thesis is vindicated—is a preliminary form of nihilism. Marxism is indeed aware of the threat of nihilism, especially in the form of fascism; but because it opposes nihilism with inadequate weapons, it is already on the way to becoming its victim. Only through a high-handed act of resolve, whose moral passion always has a somewhat grotesque effect, can the Marxist conceal from himself and from others the abyss of nihilism which is the logical consequence of his views. Into this abyss Marxism is slipping, and there is really nothing to hold it back.

The interpretation is given content in the following manner, that the action of contemporary life with its exertions, sacrifices and sufferings should find its meaning in the goal whose attainment it serves. Here the Hegelian inheritance shows itself, and here the change introduced by the Hegelian philosophy of history has important consequences. For Marxism also the goal gives meaning to history. All its detours, contradictions and sacrifices are justified in the light of the goal. Because the world no longer stands over against God, the meaning of an individual epoch and an individual existence can no longer consist, as it still did for Ranke, in its immediate relationship to God, but only in its relationship to that final society. It must be enough for earlier ages to find satisfaction in the thought that their significance consists in being a preparation for that society.

Here, too, we are presented with a theodicy; the question is only whether it is really valid. For Marx, too, as a pupil of Hegel, the chaos of historical events, at first sight so impenetrable, sorts itself out, the advances and catastrophes order themselves from a confusion of blind accidents to a meaningful line which leads upwards—even if sporadically and not directly. "Nothing will have been in vain, all nations and classes, all individuals and ideas find their place in this worldview, every being and every matter is marked by a positive or unpositive sign, in relation to the past or to the future, marked with the sign of disgrace or sanctified by its participation in the work of history."[16] In the Hegelian teleology the individual could still know that he was affirmed and secured in the totality inasmuch as the foundation of the world was the Spirit in which he also participated; further, Hegel had in mind a picture of the whole, in which the question of the individual was answered in terms of his position in the whole. But now this justification of the individual is not given in terms of a general picture of the whole, but in terms of a future realization within time of the whole, by means of which that which preceded is justified as an earlier stage leading to this realization. Thus the question of meaning is answered in the context of the belief in progress.

But then the questions which Kierkegaard and Bielinski had already put to Hegel must be given an even sharper point. As later Dostoevsky, in *The Brothers Karamazov*, was to plead the tears of innocent suffering children, so already W. Bielinski[17] had described Hegel's "Absolute" in its relation to the individual subject as a Moloch, and rejoined "The fate of the subject, the individual, the person, is more important than the fate of the whole world, and the health of the Emperor of China (that is the Hegelian 'Absolute'). Thank you very much, Jegor Fedoritsch (Hegel)—I bow before your philosophical nightcap, but with all due reverence to your philosophical philistinism. I have the honour to inform you that if I were to succeed in climbing to the top of the ladder of evolution—I would even there seek you out to bear witness to all the victims of living conditions and of history, all the victims of chance, of superstition, of the Inquisition of Philip II, etc., etc. Otherwise I shall throw myself down head over heels from the topmost step. I do not even wish for the

[16] Aron, *Der Monat*, November, 1950, p. 182.

[17] In his letter to W. P. Botkin, 1 March, 1841, printed in *Orient und Okzident*, ed. F. Lieb, 1930, vol. 3, p. 46; cf. K. Löwith, *Von Hegel zu Nietzsche*, pp. 159f., and the remarks by L. Schestoff in the foreword to his book, *Dostojewski und Nietzsche*, Cologne, 1923.

free gift of happiness, unless I am satisfied about the fate of every single one of my blood-brothers—bone of my bone and flesh of my flesh."

We must indeed reflect that Marxism was not designed for philosophical philistines, but for fighters who were at last to compel the arid history of mankind towards a rational goal. But that does not help matters for us, since we are here asking the question of meaning with the seriousness with which it is raised by the fullness of meaning of the gospel. Only a fighter can take satisfaction in that future condition of a rational society, and even he can only do so when and in so far as he is able actively to contribute to the future, and thus to earn credit by so doing, and consciously to appropriate the future in his life. But this source of significance does not extend to cover acts which have nothing to do with the struggle for the future. This source of meaning, of justification and condemnation, is like a net of too wide a mesh; it leaves many acts of life in irrelevant indifference, for example the world of inner experience and of so-called private relationships. Either the fighter is entirely absorbed in political work —or he lives alongside of it still in a realm which is not comprehended and thus not disciplined by the avowedly universal goal. A political world-view is not capable of giving an all-embracing significance and with it discipline (theologically expressed, sanctification) to life—or only does so by absorbing life wholly into itself. This explains the two types of life of political fighters with a total political world-view; either the ambiguous phenomenon of discipline in the realm of politics, and an undisciplined private life, or the suppression of all extra-political private life.

But this source of meaning reaches its limits at once also when a man is excluded from action for the goal and becomes useless through illness, age, or the like, or has no share in the action from the first, for similar and other reasons. Then no element in the theory protects him from being treated as mere material to be used in building the future. Such a

117

this-worldly eschatology can give no foundation for the dignity of man today as a person, and the concept of meaning, because it cannot be understood as grounded in the affirmation of man by an enduring love, must be equated with that of the end and the means to an end. This is the point where Marxism has placed itself in the greatest danger, for it began as a militant humanism aiming at a future society which should be a free society, i.e. as the Communist Manifesto states, "an association in which the free development of each is the condition of the free development of all". Without an adequate definition of the meaning for life of "each", the meaning of freedom cannot be adequately defined either. Since in the centre of the Marxist world-view there is a contradiction between promise for man and misunderstanding of man as a person, as an "end in himself" (Kant), it continually falls into contradiction between the humanist tendency and the unscrupulous justification of the means by the end.[18]

The secularization of Christian eschatology which Marxism has consciously undertaken, has not only swept aside a mythological context, but at the same time the specific source of meaning which in conjunction with the outlook of the future alone constituted "Christian humanism", the allocation of personal value as an end-in-itself to all men without exception, and to every individual man. Christian eschatology also anchors the meaning of the present in the future, it also bases "the infinite value of the human soul", the value of everything "that bears a human face", not in the qualities of man, in an indestructible kernel of nobility, in his participation in timeless intellect, but in the movement of God (founded in the story of the coming of Jesus Christ) towards the inevitable victory of his love. Because this history is thought of in terms of God's confrontation of his creation,

[18] In the field of literature this finds expression, for example, in the contradiction between the solutions given to similar problematic situations in Bertolt Brecht's play, *Die Massnahme*, and in the popular novel of the German Democratic Republic by B. Apitz, *Nackt unter Wölfen*.

nothing here falls under the table, i.e. the sufferings of the individual victims of history are not trivialized in the light of the future consummation, the Christian message gives the answer to the problem of a theodicy, and the question and the accusation against the Lord of history included in the problem. It does so in three connected propositions. 1. In the Kingdom of God there is no distinction between earlier and later, there are not some who are only at a material and a pre-paratory stage to happiness, and others who enjoy it; in the blessedness of the Kingdom of God all have an equal share. 2. The question and accusation addressed to God on the score of the sufferings of history will stick in the throats of the accusers in face of the Cross, i.e. when confronted by the knowledge that the Lord of history himself has to carry the greater burden of history. 3. Blessedness will consist in the life and rule of love between the Creator and the creatures, i.e. in the knowledge that they are loved by the creator, in their thankful gratitude, and so also in trust in him which does not demand any book-keeping, but gladly and trustfully acknow-ledges the mystery of God and his rule. But this is already possible in faith. Future and present thus do not stand exclus-ively over against each other as pre-history and end-history; they do not stand in a pure succession of chronological time —Τῇ γὰρ ἐλπίδι ἐσώθημεν (Rom. 8:24) is not only, as Luther translates it, meant as a limitation. "So we are now saved, *but* in hope"—but at the same time it already fills the present. "In (or 'with' or 'in the power of') hope we were saved." This hope can really save in the present, in it every individual is now already secure. That is an incredible promise of meaning which cannot be so easily forgotten. It is effective as a standard even where its sphere has been left behind. Every other message that undertakes to replace it, to surpass it, or at least to provide a substitute for it, is exposed to its standard. It must not only make the rigorous challenge that man has to sacrifice himself for the whole, for the future, etc., it must not only claim that this gives meaning to his life, it must rather show how far the coming fulfilment is so qualified, that it is already able to give meaning to the present. Thus the question once put by Arthur Koestler must not remain unanswered, how far the undisturbed good fortune of the self-development of future generations of sheep can be a consolation for the sheep that are now being slaughtered.[19] The question of meaning must not be shouted down by ethics. It is good to claim that man should sacrifice himself for the life of future generations—but only so long as the claim is not made that this is the answer to the question about the meaning of his existence. But this is a question which all men have continually to face, whether we use the word "meaning" or not. So long as this question is acute—and it is acute as long as men go on living—religion has its place. That the connection between religion and the question of meaning has never been thought out in the Marxist theory of religion—much less the special significance of the Christian message—is one of Marxism's greatest weaknesses. For this reason rationalists who put their faith in science and

[19] Schiller had asked a similar question in his *Ideen zu einer allgemeinen Geschichte in weltbürgerlicher Absicht* (Collected Works, 1904ff., 12th volume, p. 24): ". . . and in what relationship would we stand then to the past and the future age of the world, if the development of human nature made such a sacrifice necessary? We would have been the thralls of humanity, we would have done slave labour for it for some centuries, and stamped the shameful marks of this servile time upon crippled nature, so that a later generation in blissful idleness could await its moral health, and develop the free growth of its humanity!" On this whole question, cf. L. Landgrebe, "Das Problem der Dialektik" in *Marxismusstudien*, 3rd Series, 1960, p. 62: "If now in Marx the human species takes the place of Absolute Spirit, so the same conditions must hold here for the relation of the single individual to the Universal as for Hegel. The self-realization of the single individual can only mean his absorption without remainder in the process of the realization of the species. For this alone, as the substance in all becoming, is the one thing that happens for its own sake, and that means, that the individual as individual can only have the right to his existence, insofar as he serves the attainment of this goal. He has only so far a claim to his freedom, and to recognition by the species. The right of the species crushes the right of man as a personal individual."

satisfy themselves with the arid formula defining religion as a prescientific form of world-interpretation and world-domination, will time and again be surprised by the virulence of religion, which will rather allow "reason" to die out than die out itself.

What is alleged by Marxism to be the meaning of history, and consequently, of the individual life, is, condensed in the form of an answer, the failure to give an answer, the admission—not only in the manner of the agnostics, that no answer is known, but the admission that the godlessness of the world forbids any better answer than this wretched one; apart from the hope that later generations, thanks to the co-operation between the innate tendency of history and conscious human action, will have a better, more human lot—there is no hope. This hope is consequently permeated with resignation and, at the same time, disturbed by anxiety, for how much can intervene and hinder the realization! And further, even the state of fulfilment, as a state within time, is a transitory one, and will again be replaced by periods of decline.[20] This life has indeed not more to offer than this even at the best! That may indeed be the case, but how can one claim to meet it with anything better than Stoic resignation? What an illusion to believe that this hope will be able permanently to conceal its secret hopelessness!

The Problem of Evil

Too restricted a view of reality is also, in the last place, shown when, as is fitting in the case of a doctrine proclaiming a total liberation, we ask for its outlook on evil.

---

[20] A thought that disturbed, not Marx, but Charles Fourier, because the latter saw clearly that the end-state must have duration, if its prospect was to take the place of the Christian hope. He helped himself out by means of the inept device of prolonging the culminating stage which he heralded; 5,000 years in ascent, and 5,000 in descent, but 35,000 years of the period of harmony, and of these, not less than 8,000 at the highest level of happiness (cf. T. Ramm, *Die grossen Sozialisten*, p. 324).

Often the opinion is expressed by the representatives of both sides, that in contrast to the pessimistic estimate of man in Christianity, as subject to original sin, all socialism is based on the faith that man is good.[21] For Marxism this only holds true with a very significant modification; contemporary man in the class-society is by no means good, but so bad that he only deserves to be liquidated. But this badness of his had a historical origin, and is to be historically overcome. Even this statement in itself does not yet conflict with the Christian conception, since according to the latter also, the badness of man is a secondary and historical character, contrasting with his primary character as a good creation of God. The parallel between the Marxist theory of history and the Christian history of salvation has been often remarked.[22] The first sentence of the Communist Manifesto, "The history of all society hitherto is a history of class-struggles", does not hold absolutely for *all* history; it does not hold for the Communist primitive society, nor for the soon-expected final society. Now Marx and Engels see the reason for the transition from primitive Communism to the class-age in the division of labour and the resultant private property. In Engels[23] the remark occurs once that the division of labour gave all sorts of unlovely instincts (avarice, violence, egoism) the occasion to develop, but that this was necessary in order to transcend the first, original stage of production. Whence these "instincts" suddenly emerge, he does not say. He avoids going into this because a rational ground is needed to explain the above-mentioned transition. It is needed in order to be able to promise also the coming transition as one which can be rationally organized. As a social change modified man for

[21] E.g. W. Sombart, *Der Sozialismus und die soziale Bewegung*, 1919, 7th Edn., pp. 34f.

[22] Cf. F. Delekat, "Vom Wesen des Geldes, Eine theologische Marx-analyse" in *Ev. Th.*, 1950, pp. 289–308. *Marxismusstudien*, 1st Series, 1953, pp. 54–76.

[23] "Der Ursprung der Familie . . ." in K. Marx—F. Engels, *Ausge-wählte Werke*, East Berlin, 1951, vol. 2, pp. 236f.

the worse, so a social change can modify him again for the better. By such a reduced view of evil—rationally explained in terms of external conditions of life, and reduced to the instinct for possession, thus identified with asocial elements—the illusion can arise that it can be removed by social alterations. And conversely, the absolute value ascribed to the significance of social alterations requires a reduced view of evil. For the Christian view evil is not capable of rational explanation—the old question of the philosophers, *unde malum?* (whence does evil come?), is not theoretically answerable. Evil is seen as the *mysterium iniquitatis* (the mystery of iniquity), even as the "impossible possibility" (Barth), as the unfathomable and underivable decision of man, first of all a decision against his own origin, against the divine giver, and in the light of this—but inevitably following on from it—also the decision against his neighbour. This decision is identical with the loss of freedom, so that a self-liberation is no longer possible. And this gives to mundane possibilities of improvement and education, which yet must not be denied or underestimated, their insurmountable limit. There is here not only a much deeper insight into man's plight, but also (profundity as such would be no sign of truth), a much more sober one. The façade of respectability is not valueless for our social life together, but the man who lets himself be deceived by it, who is ignorant, theologically speaking, that the law is capable of creating a *justitia civilis* but not of the transformation of a sinner into a good man, looks on custom and hypocrisy as goodness, and stumbles from one self-deception to another. Even in the sphere of Marxism, experience has amply confirmed, not the hopes there cherished, but the old theological knowledge of the *impossibilitas legis*; the inability of the law, to realize the good which it demands. If, in Nietzsche's words, idealism is defined as the inability to bear the truth about man, then Christian faith is very much less idealistic than Marxism.

CHAPTER SEVEN

The Bankruptcy of the Religion of Revolution

THE way we have taken in this discussion started with our consideration of the evils which will still remain even in the society of the future (inequality, guilt, death). Then we went on to the question of meaning, and the problem of evil. This, as we said at the beginning, should indicate the contradiction between the actually limited character of the Utopian scheme and its Messianic claim. Here is promised a fulfilment which —not only on a sceptical evaluation of the human possibilities, but also on the basis of the assertions of the theory itself—cannot be so great as it claims to be. Even to the classless society, when we consider it more closely, we shall have to apply the observation of Nestroy: "In general progress has this quality, that it appears to be much greater than it really is".[1] This quotation is not made in a spirit of ridicule, although the fact that we have discovered might elicit ridicule; the offer to thrust aside the Christian message and its eschatology as a substitute, in order to offer something better in its place, turns out itself to be a substitute in the bad sense of the word. There are, however, three reasons why this may not be stated in a spirit of ridicule.

1. It is disclosed that the Christian message is no possession

[1] Motto of Ludwig Wittgenstein's "Philosophical Investigations". For a theological estimate of the belief in progress I may refer to the old, but still equally valuable essay of Martin Kähler, "Der Menschheit Fortschritt und des Menschen Ewigkeit" in *Dogmatische Zeitfragen*, 1898, vol. I, pp. 16–45; and in addition, to G. Casalis, "Eschatologie und Fortschritt" in *Unterwegs*, Series for 1951, and to the remarks of E. Rosenstock-Huessy in *Der Christen Zukunft*, 1953, pp. 117ff.

that man can take for granted. Where the truly unprecedented and incredible promise of this faith, which therefore can only be believed, which depends on faith, that does not stand at our disposal like a rational inference—when the promise of this message is not heard, has not yet sounded forth or is misrepresented, man must make do with something else, and has at all times done so. Part of the contradiction which this message addresses to man, as it finds him, is due to its disclosure of the inadequacy and "ersatz character" of this self-help, which has to be abandoned. An insight into the paradoxical character of this promise, i.e. its miraculous character as an act of grace, must help the Christian, who sees himself laid hold of by it, to understand these different ways of contriving-to-find-significance-in-ourselves—must help him to understand modern atheism. If it is true of Marx that "Atheism is for him no problem, but something to be taken for granted",[2] then he shares in a spiritual fate of modern times that is not strange to the Christian. The latter must understand that such a fate drives men to promise to themselves more from the goal of their efforts than it can provide when realized.

2. Since this modern atheism replaces a time of notably general acceptance of Christianity, the Christian will have to ask himself what disappointments provided by himself, by his society, by the empirical Church, have caused this replacement. That this hope, which he had to represent, could be regarded as pale, nebulous, as a flowery decoration of earthly chains, as an opiate and an ideology of oppression, is a judgment on him and on his society itself, to which he must submit without sparing himself.

3. Our remarks are not directed against Marxism as a movement of social revolution, nor against its diagnosis and cure of society in so far as it can be rationally argued and rationally discussed. Their aim is rather to bring its rational

---

[2] So L. Landgrebe, "Das Problem der Dialektik" in *Marxismusstudien*, 3rd Series, 1960, p. 42.

kernel to the light of day. Thus our remarks furnish no weapons against Communism. They do not take a party line in the quarrel between it and its political opponents. They do not seek to show that its programme is impracticable, or that its execution would not be an advance, but a calamity. Nor do they intervene in the dispute between revolution and reform. Their aim is rather to put in rational terms as far as possible even this dispute, which aims at discrediting every revolutionary effort by means of the traditional doctrine of authority, a doctrine whose purpose and whose limits cannot be brought into this discussion. And precisely with this in view it must be disclosed that revolution cannot and will not in any case bring about what the "Religion of revolution", the Messianism of revolution, promises with its claim to the total fulfilment of man. Not in order to fall upon the militant Communist and compel him to give up his struggle—that may be the task of his political opponents by means of rational, empirical, and political arguments—but in order to make him more realistic and through this realism to refer him to the plane of the social and political struggle, to make him really political, it is necessary to dissuade him from competition with religion. That the programme of social revolution should still claim to satisfy the metaphysical need of meaning, that it should claim to bring about the victory of a universal world-view, and enforce metaphysical and religious decrees (for even anti-metaphysical and anti-religious negations are of course metaphysical and religious assertions), is a scandal inherited from the nineteenth century, which has various injurious effects on the true social and political endeavour of Communism. It prevents others who have reasons for holding other world-views from giving an unprejudiced consideration to the social and policital programme of Communism. (This is the ballast of anti-religious dogma for Communist propaganda in wide areas of the working-class and among the coloured peoples!) It distorts the true political issues by means of extra-political motives; it thrusts aside hindrances to the methods of the struggle for political power, which are essential to preserve human rights (the today-acknowledged Stalinist error with its "disregard for Socialist legality"), has also at least a connection with the absolute character of the world-view of Communism, and its consequent disregard for dissident views. The adherence to Messianism is not the strength of Communism as its ideologists claim, but does harm and injury to it daily.

At this point it must again be mentioned that the competition with religion into which Marxism has allowed itself to be enticed does indeed compel it to make its immoderate claim, but that the immanent self-limitation of its vision of the future, which contradicts this, makes also possible another, more limited, self-understanding, without, as its representatives fear, taking away its dynamic from it. In the few places in which Marx, for example, expresses himself on the problems of individual and community touched on above (with the exception of the lyrical eschatological statements of the Paris manuscripts), he does certainly say that the consciousness of individuals in the Communist society is "quite different" from that of earlier epochs, but this holds good only in so far as within this Communist society, in contrast with earlier societies, "the original and free development of individuals is no mere phrase" and that because these individuals through their "solidarity" and through their "universal modes of activity on the basis of the powers of production present" are not compelled to assert and develop their possibilities of life in conflict with others. This new situation certainly creates a new consciousness, a new relatedness to the community, and consequently a new kind of freedom, no longer the freedom of private reservation, asserted with difficulty in opposition to others, but a freedom such as we now already experience in the comradeship of a team. "Only in fellowship with others has every individual the means to develop his capacities on all sides, thus only in fellowship is personal freedom possible. . . . In real fellowship individuals attain their freedom in and through their association."[3] Let us assume that this situation will come, that man will succeed "in overturning all the conditions in which man is a humiliated, enslaved, forsaken, contemptible being",[4] that the Communist movement knows the way to it, and actually contributes to bring it about—then even that gives us no reason to believe that, when humanity has at last actually left its grossest irrationalities behind, the consciousness of men should have so changed that continuity with earlier times will be broken. Everything points to the probability that we earlier men would still talk the same language as these men. All the changes in the world will not make the future world exotic. Those constant factors are still there, there is still jealousy and cowardice, love and disappointed love, betrayal and failure, joy and the concern for joy, melancholy and contempt, illness, old age, and death. There is still the question of meaning, and there are still the abysses of the heart. Thus there will still be philosophy,[5] and there will continue to be "religious ideas", and the Christian fellowship will still be there—this certainty is admittedly based on the assertion of faith—*quod perpetuo mansura sit ecclesia*, that the Church will always continue (*Confessio Augustana*, art. 7), but its historical probability is no whit less than that of the Marxist prognosis, and there is by and large no reason why the gospel will have less actual relevance than it has today. We may be of the same opinion as John Stuart Mill, that the greatest part of the history of mankind has had to do with avoidable evils, and we may therefore give full approval to the removal at last of what can be removed, and the Church,

[3] *Deutsche Ideologie,* pp. 464f., 207.

[4] *Frühschriften,* p. 209.

[5] All these insights have now begun to dawn. This is what lately Adam Schaff, the spokesman of the orthodox-Marxist school among Polish philosophers, said: "Two Marxists, who start from the same general presuppositions, can represent not only two different views, but even contradictory views. In proportion as Marxism becomes the dominating theory on its basis, different problems and tendencies, which we know from the history of the discipline, will revive again in other forms. That is only too natural." *Ostprobleme,* 1961, p. 669.

however hard, as we know, it is for it to repent, may be more cautious about the misuse of its assertion that the world cannot be improved to hinder the changing of what is alterable—but the powerful reality of that-which-cannot-be-changed still stands, and will remain.[6] This has its seat both in man's environment and in himself. We must put up with it, and because of it, not only resistance and rebellion, but also patience and resignation will continue to be reckoned as among the qualities necessary for mankind. To look this fact in the face is not negative, it is not a temptation to passivity instead of activity, it is rather a help to the right activity, because it protects the latter from oscillating between *superbia* and *desperatio*, as Luther used to say, between illusionary arrogance and disillusioned despair. It is not true that sobriety paralyses action, as the Marxist obviously always fears when Christians refer to things which we cannot change by our action. It in fact protects action from the discouragement which is to be expected, by helping us to attack energetically what can be changed, without being afraid of trespassing over the boundary of what cannot be changed, because this boundary can be tolerated by the man who tolerates it in belief in that greater hope, and therefore is not compelled to shut his eyes to it. The unalterable never cancels out the meaningfulness of our actions, but always cancels out only our illusions. The "Religion of Revolution" must therefore nervously shut its eyes to it, because it is afraid of it. But it is not true that our request should be, as Wilhelm Raabe says, "Give us this day our daily illusion!". A realistic view of the boundary does not paralyse when it is "consoled". "Consolation" need no more be a sentimental word than "love". Consolation is reconciliation with the boundary—not only the resigned bitterness of having to make

6 For the following cf. H. D. Wendland, "Die Welt verändern— zur christlichen Deutung und Kritik einer marxistischen These", in *Verantwortung für den Menschen*: *Gedenkschrift für Heinrich Held*, Stuttgart, 1956, pp. 27ff., now in *Botschaft an die soziale Welt*, 1960, pp. 202ff.

do, but the affirmation of finitude as the sphere which we can fill, gratitude for the fact that we have not been given the task of saving ourselves, of achieving everything ourselves, but only a limited improvement which corresponds to our powers. The trust that the universe is better cared for in other, higher hands, makes possible this reconciliation and thanks for the limitation of our possibilities, freed from the delusion that we ourselves must give things a meaning, and from the advance that goes forward over dead bodies.

The boundaries upon which we impinge with our possibilities are mutually interconnected. They are nothing negative, as our urge towards the infinite first makes us think, but something positive. Only the recognition of them makes us capable of fellowship. When we come up against the boundaries of the unalterable, we need our fellow-man as a brother, and at the same time we learn to acknowledge him also as our boundary. But what secures our fellow-man against our transgressing the boundaries, and making him the material of our actions, our Messianism? The proclamation of man as the highest being for man, so long as this proclamation was accompanied by a theory which treated actual men in the present period of "prehistory" only as a preliminary stage to the real man of the future, gave no security against the domination of man over man. Messianism legitimates acts of violence against the present-day real man, and leaves no defence against the totalitarian temptations of power, because it gives them an ideological sanction. Our fellow-man must be acknowledged as the boundary of our transforming activity, and for this he must be revealed to us as standing in another relation which is not at our disposal. It must be shown to us that the concrete man does not belong to us, nor to my best goals, nor to society and its greatest figures. His humanity, its unassailability, is secured when he belongs to a Master whom we cannot assail. That the other man belongs to God, that he is not the highest being, but creature and child of the "Highest Being"—this does not debase him, but exalts him, and secures him from my aggression. The proclamation of the godless man hands over man to the aggression of man.[7] This is what the Bible means when it proclaims as gospel that God knows the individual by name (Exodus 33:12; John 10:3; Jer. 1:5; Psalm 139:1 ff.). God's property-right over man is the contradiction of every total right of man, or an idea, or a truth, however beautiful, over a man, it is the wall which prevents the total absorption of a man by his social functions. This is of decisive importance in a time in which the progressive socialization of man threatens to suffocate man's selfhood. While Western propaganda accuses the East on this score, the same process in other forms is very speedily at work in the West behind men's backs, and with a result equally alarming. The Messianic denial of God heightens the dangers of this process, because in theory it lays low the barriers of reverence for the mystery which is latent in the relationship of every individual man to God.[8] With the rationalization of nature and history, man becomes more thoroughly manipulable. In contrast with this, the Christian message stands for our fellowman like a boundary, for this beneficent boundary, for the unassailability of every man as the decisive condition of human fellowship and its wealth.

[7] W. Wiesner, "Dialektischer Materialismus und christlicher Glaube" in *Theol. Zeitschrift,* Basle, 1961/1, p. 57. "Since only God in Jesus Christ has an absolute claim on man, neither can any man, nor society as a whole, set up an absolute dominion over a fellowman. . . . Since God alone as the Lord has a claim to the faith and the conscience of man, no man, no State, no party, no society, may bring the conscience of man into servitude by means of an allegedly absolute doctrine."

[8] This was very clearly expressed by Leon Trotsky, e.g. in his address on the nature of revolution at the yearly conference of the Sverdlov University in 1923 to the students of that day: "The revolutionary must not be afraid of deracinating, and must himself be deracinated, i.e. he must annihilate in himself and around him all subjective hindrances in the way of revolutionary acts (religion, morals, legality). *Therefore* we regard atheism, which is an element of materialism, as an indispensable constituent of a terrorist revolutionary education." (Quoted from R. Nürnberger, *Niedersächsische Vortragsreihe,* vol. 9, pp. 10f.)

The distinction between the alterable and the (positively and negatively) unalterable, is thus not a matter which a movement aiming at world-transformation can disregard. To shun it is a sign of weakness; to leave it to one's opponents is a mistake; to have to learn about it from experience is the sign of lack of realism; to postpone its consideration until later is a piece of false book-keeping. For this reason the answer sometimes to be heard on the Marxist side—that in the matter of the unalterable we have to do with unfruitful "last" problems which we should neglect in favour of the solution of "first" problems which are soluble by us—is an evasion. Firstly this separation between "first" and "last" questions is quite untenable, since the "last" questions are nothing else than the questions of principle. And these are the primary questions, in relation to which in any case we have, from the first, in one way or the other, consciously or unconsciously, always taken up our position, when we apply ourselves to the "soluble" questions. For this reason indeed Marxism itself has always been opposed to a mere pragmatism, and has held that commitment to a position in relation to the last questions, in the form of a general theory, was necessary. The problem is only whether the connection which the party makes between "first" and "last" questions can be secured by setting up a general theory of monopolistic authority, which claims to be derived from science. A limitation to the "first" practical questions of social life might be conceivable, which did not indeed isolate these in practice from the fundamental questions, but regarded the connection between both kinds of questions as an ever new epistemological task, to which all have to contribute.

And this would be a task which would be the subject of ever new co-operation and approach in the intellectual life of a society. This would mean the affirmation of a "pluralism" in intellectual life, without which the Marxist picture of the freedom of the individual in the communist society becomes an unthinking phrase. In the second place, just that distancing of the "first" questions from the "last" indicates such a self-limitation of Marxism as is already to be observed today in many non-Communist Marxists, and which Marxism-Leninism has still to achieve. In the non-committal answer the necessity of such a distinction is obviously conceded, and this means that the universal claim of the revolution is discredited.

That the Communist society of the future has only a limited solution of human problems to offer, is conceded by a brochure of the S.E.D. on the questions of religion, without sufficient clarity about the consequences of this concession. Its author, Hermann Scheler,[9] attacks statements of Ludwig Landgrebe, who had asked in an essay on "Hegel und Marx"[10] the justified question whether the growth of rationality prophesied for the future by Marx meant that man in an "existence which has now reached an equilibrium of repose" has become so satiated and unquestioning that he has no more need of "reflecting about the why and whither of his existence". H. Scheler answers this with the double question:

1. "If it will give comfort to the theologian—even in socialism men will reflect about the why and the whither of their life." But, he says, there is no reason why "in such a really human world" (i.e. in a world in which the relationships between man and man and man and nature are, as relationships shaped by men themselves, "perfectly transparent and comprehensible")[11] "the thoughts of man about the why and the whither of his life should be religious ideas and not scientific thoughts about the natural and sociological connections of human life.

2. It is "flagrant contradiction" to think that man is only

[9] *Die Stellung des Marxismus-Leninismus zur Religion*, East Berlin, 1957, p. 29.

[10] *Marxismusstudien*, 2nd Series, 1954, p. 52.

[11] This expression of Scheler's stems from Marx: "The religious reflection of the real world can only disappear so soon as the conditions of practical workaday life day after day represent to men transparently rational relationships to one another and to nature. The form of the social life-process, i.e. of the material process of production, strips off only its mystic cloud-veil, as soon as it stands forth as the product of freely associated men under well-planned control." *Das Kapital*, vol. 1, Berlin, 1957, pp. 84f.

capable of creative development of his spiritual powers under the burden of servitude and the deformities of the class society, but not in the unrestricted freedom of the socialist society with its removal of all alienation.

To this in my opinion we must answer: 1. There is no reason why the removal of alienation, the transparency of a man's relationships, should make his question about the why and the whither easier than before. Has man himself, in Scheler's opinion, become completely transparent and comprehensible? Nor is there any reason why men should not continue to answer these questions, as previously, in very different ways, and among these, by means of "religious ideas". Scheler calls these "supersensual, fantastic religious ideas", and thus betrays so vague and antiquated a conception of what "religious ideas" are about, that he hardly shows by this his competence to take part in the debate in the twentieth century. He seems to be unconscious of the burden, the fearful burden, of these questions, he obviously regards them as a leisure pursuit of the man of the future. But just because the distress caused by these questions is not lessened by the changes of society, their answer, and the attitude we take to them, is not prejudiced by this change, and it is therefore impossible to make prophetic statements about them. But one thing certainly can be said in advance; science (in the sense of our modern concept of science, which indeed Scheler also intends), will in the future be just as little able to throw light as it does today on the why and the whither of existence, and pass a verdict on "religious ideas". To give it this task is a piece of old-fashioned folly which ought not to be trotted out to grown people who understand something of science.

Scheler's second counter-question, however, gives us the opportunity of parrying a misunderstanding to which, in its turn, our reference to the significance of the continuing burden of inequality, guilt, and death is liable. This is not intended as an exhaustive formula explaining the rise of "religious ideas" (in the sense of the old saying *timor fecit deos* (fear made the gods); its purpose is not to represent God as a mere helper in need, and thus as a product of need, as if joy and good-fortune did not also lead to worship and create situations for faith; least of all was it intended to resist the abolition of suffering and servitude with the argument of the blessedness of suffering. Its target is the Marxist prognosis of the extinction of religion through the disappearance of need, and, in rebuttal of this, it points out types of need that will continue. Beyond this, it certainly does contain the question whether an ingredient of pressure and need is not actually necessary to man for the development of his powers, and whether in a conception of happiness which denies this, that kind of experience is forgotten, out of which, for example, the Hegelian Dialectic took its origin.

The claim made by the eschatological promise of Communism is total, but in contradiction to this its content is limited. The doctrine fails to give an adequate interpretation and evaluation of human personal being,[12] but in reality, on the other hand, this person is very much on the map. In theory, reality should be made rational through revolutionary action, but in contradiction to this, it is the reality, which by its opposing factors forces the revolution to give up its hybrid claim, and, as far as possible, makes it reasonable. In life itself the individual bestirs itself, and compels the recognition of its reality, as this perpetually unfathomable, incalculable being, centred in itself, and yet continually transcending itself, a being which exists in social relationships, and is yet in tension with these relationships. It manifests its reality in attractive and unattractive ways, altruistically and selfishly, in love of neighbour and in sex, in sacrifice and in greed, in conscience and frivolity, in performance of duty and in life-anxiety. Under its pressure Soviet literature is revising

---

[12] Helmut Kuhn goes too far when he says, in an essay on M. Merleau-Ponty, "No one attains to the inner sanctuary of the Marxist religion who has not first divested himself of the one fundamental concept of Greek metaphysical and Christian origin, the concept of the person, which is concerned, in its knowledge and action within time, about an eternal gain, its 'salvation', and which thereby transcends in dignity of being the temporal reality of society." (*Philosophisches Jahrbuch der Görresgesellschaft*, 62nd year, 1953, p. 331.) In my opinion this goes too far, it brings Marxism under a most extreme formula, which frees it from the inner contradiction from which its humanism—luckily!—suffers.

its patterns, and giving to it more and more expression, the Marxist philosophy must concede that hitherto it has neglected the problems of personality, and is trying to face up to them.[13] Thus the greater the progress in the realization of the programme, the more the reproach of outsiders that Communism denies the personal character of man, is being transformed into the question, arising within the party, as to whether in theory and practice sufficient account has been taken of human individuality. The realization is dawning that it will not be possible permanently to account for disturbing phenomena with the face-saving explanation that they are "capitalistic left-overs". It is being realized that the relationship between individual and society can never be solved once and for all by an ordering of society, but is an ever-new individual and collective task, for which an existent order provides the context and the material, and also, admittedly, a sometimes better, sometimes worse support, according as it fosters social or anti-social tendencies. The unchanging needs, constraints and conflicts are asserting themselves, their restraint and official suppression was a constraint which took its revenge by the atrophy of the human element and could not to be permanently continued—and all the less so, the more the changes were accomplished which were claimed to be the justification of that restraint.

The reality is more complex than it was in theory predicted to be, even the Socialist reality. The factors which bring disenchantment to Messianism are manifold. The disappointments which accompany realization, the prosaic character of daily work, make visible the gap between the gospel proclaimed and what is attainable. The absolute formulas which had been employed no longer correspond to the content of the future which is now becoming visible. The time of Messianic

[13] Cf. the significant essays of the Polish party theoreticians, Adam Schaff, "Philosophie vom Menschen" in *Hinter dem Eisernen Vorhang*, May and June, 1961, and A. Buchholtz, *Der Kampf um die bessere Welt*, Stuttgart, 1961.

136

expectation is passing away. The elements which had been united in the "religion of revolution" are being dissolved into their component parts. These are, on the one hand, the impulse of faith with which the workers of the proletariat encountered their misery, and which had given their life a new content, the stimulating function of Utopianism, the ethic and the passion of an obligation to the whole of humanity which Marxism had set over against the mammonism of the bourgeoisie and its hypocritical idealism. And, on the other hand, the arrogance of self-redemption and worship of the world as God, which undertook to set man on God's throne, a place which he was not made to fill.

The realities of the era of struggle exercised pressure towards the union of a programme of social revolution and a universal world-view with an atheistic orientation; the realities of the epoch of realization exercise pressure towards the severance of these two things, which were never really logically united, though their unity had always been asserted by the party. We recall once more the statement of Georg Klaus: "With the superstructure only theories are liquidated which do not adequately reflect the objective reality, but are merely the ideological projection of the interests of a ruling class".[14] It was an illusion and a limitation of the Marxist criticism of ideology to believe that only ruling classes were interested in an ideologically distorted picture of reality, while dominated classes on the other hand were interested in the undistorted reality itself. The struggle, too, needs its adjusted picture of reality, and even militant groups produce an ideology which projects their interests. For this reason M. Reding is thoroughly justified in asking[15] whether the connection between revolutionary and anti-religious struggle is

[14] *Jesuiten, Gott, Materie,* p. 124.
[15] *Der politische Atheismus,* p. 169. Also in his lecture, "Marxismus und Atheismus" in *Universitätstage der Freien Universität,* Berlin, 1961, pp. 160–8.

understandable as a product of the conditions of the nine-teenth century, conditions which only in part still hold good for the twentieth century. The "liquidation" of theories which no longer fit the new situation, especially since the change of the basis, must then involve also the traditional Marxist theory of religion. The latter is thus once more confronted with the problem of religion, which it believed it had irrevocably left behind it. The discussion within the party must concern itself more and more frequently with this phenomenon; it can no longer disregard its vitality even within Socialist society, and inevitably approaches the two questions: 1. Is it a part of the continuing nature of religion to be a superstructure of class-society? 2. Is it a part of the continuing nature of Communism to be atheistic and anti-religious as a requirement of the party?

An interesting document is the report of such a discussion which took place in the editorial offices of the Warsaw news-paper *Nova Kultura*, on the 7th of November 1957, and in which the leaders of Polish Marxism, among them the Min-ister for Education, W. Bienkovski, and the philosopher L. Kolakovski, took part.[16] The participants were still united in the dogmatic conviction that Marxism and the religious atti-tude are mutually exclusive because science and religion are mutually exclusive. They were puzzled by the fact that neither the setting up of Socialism in Poland nor the anti-religious agitation, nor the spread of scientific education had made appreciable inroads on Polish Catholicism, and they discussed in a spirit of self-criticism the reasons for this failure, and various proposals for the suppression of religion. Only one of them, the philosopher and sociologist Jan Strzelecki, had the idea that the mistake might lie with the unquestioning accept-ance of the traditional theory of Marxists concerning religion,

[16] In German under the title, "Diskussion über Säkularisierung" in *Hinter dem Eisernen Vorhang*, October, 1958; on L. Kolakovski's further development, cf. his "Kleinen Thesen de Sacro et Profano" in *Hinter dem Eisernen Vorhang*, September, 1961, and in a new version, in *Frankfurter Heften*, November 1961.

and said: "The greatest service which the revolution has done to the Church is nothing more, and nothing less, than the fact of social revolution." The Church, he continued, had thereby in the eyes of the broad masses lost the character of an institution bound to an exploiting order of society. "This in no way lessens its influence, but, on the contrary, increases it. For this reason the more astute fathers of the Church, who know this, have no fear of the Socialist order." This had brought the Church nearer to the masses of the people, and the dialectic of the social revolution had thereby decidedly brought it advantages.

"If in a certain defiance of the previous speeches, and with the ironic pleasure of the philosopher, I underline the influence of the gift which the realization of the revolution has given to the Church, the influence which it has upon the socio-ideological situation in which we all live and act, I do so, because I am haunted by the stubborn thought, that the dialectical thinking, i.e. keeping pace with the fluid, capricious reality, which runs counter to all systems, lays further obligations upon the circle of the heirs of revolutionary thinking. Continued insistence on contradictions which were formulated in a prehistoric manner, is not, in my opinion, characteristic of this kind of thinking. . . . The man who pays no regard to this thinks and plans his actions in a situation that does not exist. In a word, what is happening with us is not a process of polarization, but one of approximation of the social and ethical ideals of Catholicism and Socialism. For this reason I am incomparably more interested in the problem of tolerance in the system of the dictatorship of the proletariat, than in the struggle waged in the name of rationalistic obduracy. For this reason I allowed myself some irony in relation to certain speeches."

In connection with the contemporary discussion about "Liberalizing tendencies" in Communism, the question about a possible change in its attitude to religion has a central place. Such a change, which today is still remotely distant, but which

139

is already suggested by the historical development, would imply a self-limitation of Communism which would have fruitful results on the whole of intellectual life in its territories, a truly creative "further revolution" of which it gladly describes itself as capable, with the often-quoted saying of Lenin that Marxism is "not a dogma, but a direction for action". This revision of its tradition could not of course mean an official turning of the party to religion, or even to Christianity, but a recognition that the relation to religion was a private matter, such as befits the nature of the modern State and modern society. These words "recognition as a private matter" show at once that a very profound revision would be involved. For the division between private person and *citoyen* was made by the young Marx the special reproach of bourgeois society, and he aimed at transcending it, since it only contributed to the reserves "of the limited, self-limited individual" the conservation of "the egoistic person".[17]

A "private" sphere in which also religious convictions can be conserved, is therefore to be actually annihilated by Socialism. But in this Marxist conception, the private sphere is only appraised as an egoistic private sphere, and the relation between individual and community only solved by the dissolution of the individual in the community. Thus this estimation of the private sphere as illegitimate is altogether a part of the "religion of revolution", with which, as Delekat rightly says, "anthropology turns again into theology". As Communism today in the Soviet Union is not able in other matters to avoid modifying the predictions of Marx (e.g. in the retention of the money market, private property, and the division of labour even in the Communist society), so also it is in process of giving a new positive value to the sphere of private

[17] In his essay "Zur Judenfrage", *Frühschriften,* pp. 192f. The significance of this essay for the problem of atheism, its descent from Rousseau and Hegel, and its theological problems, are dealt with in the discussion of F. Delekat: "Begriff und Probleme des politischen Atheismus bei Karl Marx" in *Stat Crux, dum volvitur orbis, Festschrift für Bischof Hanns Lilje,* Berlin, 1959, pp. 171–87.

matters and the private interest. Although the sound which the word "private" derives from its origin (*privare*, to rob) makes it suspect to both the Marxist and the Christian, yet this must not prevent its use to describe the sphere of the individual's own decision, which is in no way alien to the interests of society, but for which he alone is responsible, and which the community must set free for him. In this sense, says Delekat,[18] rightly, the demand for a separation of State and religion rests on the Christian theological insight that God's rule, which has been revealed in Jesus Christ, cannot be politically realized. If, thus understood, the legal disestablishment of the religious sphere as a private matter is to be affirmed on Christian grounds, so also the way of the Communist party towards the legal affirmation of religion as a sphere of private choice, will not be harder or more unthinkable for it to follow than it was for the Church to follow on the way from the Middle Ages to modern times.[19]

[18] Delekat, op. cit, p. 187.
[19] Similar thoughts are today expressed by many observers, e.g. by W. Kolarz in an essay on "Recent Soviet Attitudes Towards Religion" in *Ostprobleme*, 1957/26, p. 911: "There is no reason why following on criticism of other outmoded dogmas, there should not also be a revision of the traditional, monotonously repeated Soviet standpoint in the question of religion. Many Communists could argue that there was absolutely no necessary connection between the erection of a new social order and the demands of the anti-God movement. They could then further cite the fact that the definition of religion as 'a leftover of capitalism in the brains of men' was unhistorical, since religion, and in particular the Christian religion, existed already in pre-capitalist times. One would be much more justified in pointing out a 'capitalist' or at least 'bourgeois' *provenance* for militant Soviet atheism than for religion, since its propagandists have borrowed many of their arguments from the 'bourgeois' rationalists of the eighteenth and nineteenth centuries. If the Communists wished to break with atheism, in order to use their own arguments, better answering to their way of thinking, it would not be difficult to find them. Robespierre describes atheism as 'aristocratic', why should not the successors of Stalin list it as a 'bourgeois' element"? Suggestions of a similar kind also in Delekat, op. cit. at the beginning of page 186. Cf. the conversations with Soviet intellectuals on religious questions in Irmgard Gröttrup's memories of Russia, *Die Besessenen und die Mächtigen*, Stuttgart 1958, pp. 81f.

Whether after such trenchant revision Communism can still be called "Communism" is merely an academic question. What belongs to the unvarying elements of Communism can today hardly be decided with certainty for the future, since the evolution after Stalin's death, and the division of the movement into several types of Communism has already provided us with several surprises. The question whether atheism and Messianism belong to the "essence" of Communism presupposes that we have here to do with an entity in which we can distinguish objective and timeless essence from accidental appearance, substance from accidents. In all historical movements this is a matter of the utmost difficulty. In our connection we only need to remind ourselves what different kinds of report would be given about *The Essence of Christianity* by Feuerbach, by a theologian of his time, and by a theologian of today, in addition to which we would have to reckon with confessional differences of interpretation, such a report is thus neither independent of its time, nor independent of personal decision, and even the question as to the constant elements in the different reports could not be given a unanimous answer, and would, in addition, by no means result in a minimum objective statement as to essentials. Historical movements only live by continually redefining themselves— and further, by continually redefining their continuity, their connectedness through the ages. Many opponents of Communism are at one with its present leaders in holding that the Messianic absolute claim, the unity of politics, social structuring, and universal world-view; the unity of socialism, atheism and Dialectical Materialism, belong to its essence. But we cannot accept such a high-handed claim to dispose of the future. What the representatives of a movement wish to do, and what they can do, are different things. Even Communism is not the subject of history, as it would fain be, but is driven along with other forces in its stream, the object of its manifold influences. Today, for a number of great, gifted, and youthfully vigorous peoples it is the form of their life. They cannot get behind it, and they cannot step out of it. They can only make of it something useful for themselves. Not only does it make something of them, but they make something of it. What the result of this mutual influence will be, is still absolutely open. In these peoples there are living religious traditions, religious communities and Christian congregations. They, too, according to the measure of their vitality, are influencing factors. In the manner in which they participate in the life of society, at one and the same time collaborating with the new orders, and refusing to acknowledge the atheistic framework of these orders, they achieve a separation of the reputedly inseparable unity of socialism and atheism, and in their life exemplify a demythologized socialism, in whose direction they must wish to see that they also, the Communists, will some day follow. Whether the influence of the factors working in this direction, of which they are themselves one, will be strong enough to assert itself against the power of the traditional doctrine to maintain itself, is undecided. In fact the realization of the socialist society, as the young Marx wrote in his Paris manuscripts, is "a harsh and long-enduring process". For this very reason we must not do Communism, as we have known it hitherto, the honour of assuming that its hitherto doctrinaire self-understanding will have the permanence that it predicts. Instead of this we must seize hold of the element of truth in its concept of development, and apply this to itself—and also to religion, in contrast with the static conception which it is accustomed to use in teaching about religion. If we know history as the sphere of change and the common life of men, and men's reciprocal influence upon each other, if we confess the living God as the Lord of history, and see our place in the community of men and nations for which we share responsibility, and to whose evolution we contribute by our behaviour, then there will vanish that shadow of finality, hopelessness and unalterability with which an avowedly timeless doctrine oppresses and paralyses us, and under whose influence we

F   143 only expect that the actions of men will logically follow from their teaching. If we only see Communism statically, pinned down to the law under which it made its debut, then we shall really see it as godless, and shall know from the start what it is, and what it can become, and what it cannot. Because God is, therefore the future is open, and therefore we have not to do with ossified essences, with metaphysical entities, but with human beings, whose future ways may yet be surprising for themselves.

CHAPTER EIGHT

Christian Encounter with Atheism

Hope and Repentance

THE hope which echoed in the last sentences is not based on impeccable evidence, it rests on Christian faith. It is therefore not a prognosis. In place of the hoped-for slackening of the bond between socialism and Messianism, there may come a tautening of it. A turn for the worse is possible in the East, as it is in all parts of the world. It is a part of Christian faith both to be prepared for this, and to make a resolute contribution towards a turn for the better. But for the latter the knowledge of the prospects is important, and knowledge of the points of contact in the doctrine in question, and also of factors which point in the same direction. It is one thing to point out such possibilities, it is a different thing to put out optimistic prognoses.[1]

Christian hope does not gloss over the existing contradictions, but sees them "in hope". The knowledge of the acuteness of the contradictions hinders hope just as little as it helps it. Both together are needed to provide the right method of encounter which is enjoined on the Christian who confronts communistic atheism.

For this reason, before we give a concluding picture of this method of encounter, we must once more state concisely what has proved to be its inner motive (apart from its external

[1] This point may be expanded and emphasized in answer to the essay of H. Thielicke, "Studie zum Atheismus-Problem" in *Zeitschrift für evangelische Ethik*, 1960, 3, pp. 129–36 (reprinted in *Spannungsfelder der evangelischen Soziallehre*) ed. F. Karrenberg and W. Schweitzer, Hamburg 1960, p. 202f., in which the position represented here is described as "Interpretation A". I can agree with the theses with which the Study ends.

experience of empirical religion and Christianity): the coupling of atheism and Messianism in the "religion of revolution" means: 1. The Messianism represents the apparent victory over the crisis into which atheism leads when it is accepted as a matter of course, as an inherited cultural and historical destiny. 2. The atheism follows the Messianism because the avowal of the latter that man can save himself is in conflict with faith in God. Thus the one confirms the other: because God does not exist, a world must be constructed, first in thought, and then in reality, in which man does not need God, and so no longer regrets God's non-existence. "The world is self-sufficient" means: since only the world exists it must be self-sufficient—and when there are men who cry, "The world is not enough for us", then we must create a form of the world in which the revolt of such idealists, Christians, etc. dies out as an absurdity. On the other hand: because this man has now decided to see his dignity in not requiring God, and can come to fulfilment without God, therefore he must also show that God does not exist. The consequence is: (a) In order to provide consolation for the preceding atheism, Messianism demands the superfluity of God both for explaining the world and for providing a meaning for life. "The world is self-sufficient" (G. Klaus). For only then does the revolution offer a completely valid, or even a superior substitute for him.[2] (b) Over and above the superfluity of God, care must be taken—in case men are not satisfied with this fulfilment and are therefore tempted to turn back to faith in God—to see that God is excluded, that his reality is impossible. With this purpose modern science is transformed into a closed system of immanence, i.e. what has a methodic

[2] Characteristically e.g. J. Dietzgen, in his "Pulpit Addresses", *Die Religion der Sozialdemokratie*, Berlin, 6th Ed., 1903: "The Saviour of modern times is called labour" (p. 6). "In the economic society lives the Saviour who can free us from bodily harm" (p. 7). "The cultivated human society is the Highest Being, in which we have *faith*; in its fashioning in a social-democratic form rests our *hope*. Only it will make real the *love*, about which religious visionaries have hitherto only sentimentalized" (pp. 16f.).

significance is given now a dogmatic-ontological meaning[3] (the disregard of transcendent references of mundane being, the explanation of world-phenomena in immanent terms, the causal explanation of transitions, the infinity of the world in past and future time, i.e. the principles of conservation, the principle of the unity of the world). That the whole system is not based on knowledge, as it claims, but on a decision and an act of faith, that it consequently is "one of the secular forms of faith in the modern post-Christian age"[3a] should by now be evident.

When we now speak of the Christian manner of encounter, we are, in so doing, presupposing a fact which will be incredible for the Marxist who thinks in the manner above described—a fact best explicable in psycho-pathological terms—that there are not only Christian men, but they will continue to exist, not in dwindling quantities, but permanently, not only thanks to their success in cutting themselves off from the socialist society and the Marxist argumentations, but existing with open minds in the midst of this society, going through these argumentations—not withdrawing from their questions, but facing up to them—and then unflinchingly adhering all the more cheerfully and emphatically to the Christian message, as to the newly acknowledged and verified truth. We do not describe here the life-encounter which will then be necessary, but refer only to the significance which the authentic existence of a Christian community has for the necessary and overdue reorientation of Communism on the religious question. It is not the only factor which exercises pressure in this direction, but it contributes, negatively and positively; negatively—by its very existence, by which it refutes the expectation of its demise, by its openminded attitude to reason and science, by means of which it refutes the dogma of the incompatibility of faith

---

[3] Cf. "Skizze einer marxistischen Ontologie" in Klaus, *Jesuiten, Gott, Materie*, pp. 152f.
[3a] Wiesner, op. cit. (p. 120, note 7), p. 54.

and science, by its steadfast refusal to concede to social life that absolute value, to Dialectical Materialism that convincing power, and to the Communist party that infallibility and authority, in which the surrounding community is indoctrinated. Thus it refutes the religion of revolution's confidence in victory.

It contributes positively by its loyal and reliable co-operation in the life of society, by its break with bad Christian traditions, by its new demonstration of a Christianity taken in earnest, and thus continually proves the possibility of energetic activity in society without atheism and dialectical materialism, and, beyond this, causes to be felt in its environment an atmosphere of brotherly and free trust which no socialism by authoritarian order can realize.[4] It must win from its faith the inner freedom to judge its own history relentlessly under the accusations of Communism, without thereby losing its glad confidence in its message, without prejudice and without anger admitting the Communists to the brotherhood in the solidarity of the godless,[5] without thereby losing its freedom and courage to make clear and emphatic contradiction.

[4] The witness of its life will thus have to demonstrate what Karl Barth in 1927 in his essay on Feuerbach formulated as the task which had been set the Church by Marx: "Should the Church not before Marx have been compelled and able to show by word and action that knowledge of *God* automatically involves and begets liberation from all hypotheses and idols? . . . Was not, and is not, the social democratic movement a mene-tekel for the Church, confronted by which it ought not so much to be filled with Pharisaic indignation as to repent? . . . It will only have peace from Feuerbach's questioning, when its ethic is fundamentally different from the cultus of old *and* new hypotheses and ideologies. Then people will believe its claim that even its God is not an illusion." *Die Kirche und die Theologie,* pp. 234f.

[5] About the origin and importance of this debated catchword of Heinrich Vogel, which has been the subject of debate in the discussion within the Church about the relation to Communism, information is given by the essay of F. W. Marquardt, "Solidarität mit den Gottlosen, Zur Geschichte und Bedeutung eines Theologumenons" in *Ev. Th.,* 1960, pp. 533–52; compare in addition Barth's early essay, "Die Theologie und der heutige Mensch" in *Zwischen den Zeiten,* 1930, pp. 387f.

Above all, this community will have to abstain from the indignation which is widely felt today in Church circles, as if atheism were a new-fangled and vicious invention of the Communists. The original thing in it is merely that here atheism is taken seriously, whereas the Church and its position in society have long depended on the fact that the world around it is indeed atheist, but would not wish to do without its Christian decoration (together with opium and fetish!). But now, on the contrary, the consequences are drawn from the already long-present atheism of natural scientists, historians, psychologists and sociologists, from the materialism of the capitalist economy, from Christianity's lack of influence on manufacture, commerce, and politics, from the schizophrenic division of man into a weekday heathen and a Sunday Christian, from the failure to implement Christian social doctrines (the gulf between white and coloured peoples, not bridged, but rather deepened by Christianity, the merely verbal reservations about the whole capitalist development!),[6] together with the actual unchurning of the great masses. This shatters the former feeling of security of the Church, which had ever and again comforted itself with the secure anchorage of Christian morals among the people, and with the respect for Christianity at least as a cultural and sentimental factor among those who were not practising Christians, and which therefore made confident claim to respect and privilege. Communism is without respect for what merely exists; it suspects that it might already belong to the past, and allows it to continue in existence only when it can prove its right to do so. This disrespectful and drastic questioning arouses alarm and indignation in the Church. This is a reaction of the ecclesiastical "flesh" (in Marxist terms, a form of the

[6] In the new social encyclical of John XXIII, *Mater et magistra*, capitalism is called "a radically perverted economic order"—but in which of the lands, in which Catholicism is the dominating world-view, has the Church of Rome even made a faint attempt at the realization of its social teaching in such a way as Communism has attempted to do with its own doctrines in the lands dominated by it?

class war). The spiritual reaction against it must consist in this, that the Church should not only admit, but inwardly accept the fact that this is how things stand, that Christianity is no longer taboo, but that every conventional status and reputation has been taken from it, and that thus it is being resolutely made the subject of discussion. The Church must take *in* the fact that the world no longer takes it *for granted*. But by the fact of ceasing to do so, the world is taking the Church with a new seriousness—or at least there is given the possibility that it will take it with a new seriousness. The Church can only inwardly accept this situation, if it understands the burden of being called in question by the world around it as God's question addressed to it, as the question addressed to it in judgment and grace by its own Lord, who wishes thereby to revive it. That the knowledge of the need of such a spiritual reaction has already made itself felt in Christian circles, can unfortunately not be maintained. What through all the Confessions finds expression in official declarations, in pulpit utterances, and in the Church press, is to a great extent only the unrepentant reaction of the flesh; and the same can be said about an adequate reconsideration of social problems in their contemporary global dimension. In my opinion there would have to be movements of a quite different order in Christianity before we could announce with Marcel Reding[7] the glad tidings of a Church attitude no longer vulnerable to Marxist criticism.

Theological Tasks

We limit ourselves here in closing, to pointing out some tasks which arise for Christian theology as a result of the Marxist criticism of religion. 1. Theology as a self-examination on the part of the Church will first have to distinguish what is valid in this criticism of religion from what is out of place, inadequate and false, which we men-

[7] *Der politische Atheismus*, pp. 236, 250, 351.

tioned in our discussion. This valid element includes both the observation of the universal sociological conditioning of religious life. and the charge that frequently religion serves the interests of the ruling classes. In the case of Christianity in particular this criticism of religion makes us aware of a transition which is repeatedly to be observed in the various epochs of Church history—a transition from a critical challenging of the existing order by the Christian message to an ideological support of the existing order. Further, it draws our attention to the singular limitation of most Christian movements of renewal (e.g. mendicant orders, Pietism, Methodism); they limit the thrust of their attack and challenge to the sphere of the private person, remain socially conservative, attacking the heathenism of individuals, but not of institutions.[8] In this is seen a limitation of Christian piety, preaching, and pastoral care in general—more strongly marked in the sphere of the Eastern Church than in the Western Churches, but valid also for the latter: the legitimate application of the gospel to the individual, the legitimate exaltation of eternal life above temporal life, of the "soul's salvation" above earthly well-being, the legitimate invitation to find consolation in patience and submission to what God has ordained, runs in fact precisely and inevitably the risk of encouraging the illegitimate modes of piety, a selfish religious desire for salvation, a flight from the world, and a fatalistic submission and the like. The Marxist accusations are a catalogue of actual Christian degenerations. One should attempt to read the theological and edifying literature of the nineteenth century with the eyes of a man like Karl Marx, before whose keen vision the trend of the times and the problems of the present and the future were evident in all their grimness, while there he could find almost nothing but

[8] Cf. on this point Karl Barth's remarks on Church History, *Church Dogmatics*, IV, 1961, 3, pp. 26–31. E. Kogon also compains that "Christian love more easily turns to any kind of help than to redress by legally based reforms". (*Frankfurter Heft*, October, 1961, pp. 666f.)

blind ignorance! This ignorance he saw to be based on a piety which he all too hastily took for the real thing. The biblical injunction to be watchful is not first of all to be directed to external opponents and temptations, but first of all to those inner dangers and possibilities of degeneration which Christian faith carries inescapably with it, and against which only a continual wakefulness can help us.

2. Christianity will have to acknowledge the weakness of traditional apologetic methods. Apologetics is necessary, if by this word the task is meant of going beyond the positive exposition of the meaning of the statements of Christian faith, to a polemical rejection of the appeal of Marxism to so-called contradictions between Christian faith and modern science, to challenge the validity of the opponent's arguments, and so on. Whether we expect much or little from this work, it cannot be wholly neglected. But we shall have to be clear on this point, that nothing can be achieved any longer by means of the traditional location of the concept of God in the gaps of natural science, by means of the assertion that the concept of God is necessary to explain the world, by means of any transformations of the old theistic proofs. All this gives the other side the opportunity of bringing the methodic atheism of modern science on the scene, and using it as a basis for dogmatic atheism. The manner in which G. Klaus in his answer to Gustav Wetter rehearses the latter's arguments, and is not forced to give way to them, shows how hopeless this whole kind of argument-spinning is. In relation both to the arguments of natural science and those of history, apologetics cannot afford to attempt to adduce supports for Christian faith, which can then be pulled around, and whose questionable character discredits Christian faith. It will rather have to content itself with removing the supports from Marxist faith, which it hopes to adduce from science, and thus to expose all the over-hasty conclusions, the unproved extrapolations, the conceptual mystifications, which are here employed. It will have to expose the blinkered attitude, the

152

dogmatist's fear of free investigation, which results from such use of science to bolster up a world-view—which is to be found now in Marxism-Leninism, as formerly in the Church. (I cite Lenin's prejudice against Einstein and the prejudice shown in the discussion of the new cosmological hypothesis, the porblem of entropy, the question of complementarity, and that of genetics, and so on.)

3. This anchoring of the concept of God as *deus ex machina* in the unexplained gaps which exist in fact or in principle is an inheritance from the connection of Christian thought with ancient metaphysics. To argue against our opponents with this sort of necessity of God was from the beginning a self-misunderstanding of Christian faith. That this argument is no longer persuasive, is a symptom of the "end of the ancient and Christian metaphysics" whose obituary Wilhelm Dilthey wrote in his "Introduction to the Mental Sciences". Like the new Protestant theology (Karl Barth, Rudolf Bultmann) and the philosophy of Heidegger, Marxism also sums up the results of this end of the great tradition of scholastic thinking in the *analogia entis*, in so far as the latter had claimed to find by speculation the rational ground of earthly being in the divine *summum ens* (most real being), and therefore conversely to pass by inference from the conditioned to the unconditioned. The presuppositions of faith concealed in these apparently rational operations have long been evident, and give Marxism the opportunity of unmasking this kind of philosophy as disguised theology. Even German idealism belongs to this tradition.[9] Whatever we are to make of Engels' crude schema for the history of philosophy (that in it there is only the alternative between an idealistic and a materialistic conception of the world) Christian theology must

[9] Hence L. Landgrebe's question to Hegel: "With this claim to the possible equation of divine thinking and human thinking, is not the Divine Reason once more thought according to the measure of what we know as our human reason, and can know from no other possible source?" ("Das Problem der Dialektik", in *Marxismusstudien*, 3rd Series, p. 40.)

see in the Marxist identification of Christianity and idealism a warning for itself not to bind the Christian faith for better or for worse to idealistic metaphysics. It does this, for example, so long as it includes the faith in creation under the inquiry about an explanation of the world. For then if the article of our faith about the creation is understood as an assertion of reason, God is a function of our self-understanding and our understanding of the world; God's existence is inferred from the existence of the world on the inducement of our need to find a causal and a teleological explanation; the creation is then a special case of the causal law, and God is the spiritual being which precedes material being as its originator. That belongs to an idealist world-view, and lies on quite another plane from the biblical belief in creation, which, e.g. in the Old Testament arises from the gracious promise of the Covenant, and thus is not the presupposition, but the consequence, of the revelation. In view of the idealistic influence on Christian thinking since the time of early Catholicism, the end of Christian metaphysics demands a thorough-going theological self-criticism, to which Marxism (with its interpretation of Christianity as a special case of idealism and idealism as a special case of theology), has given a fruitful impulse.

4. Just as little will theology identify the Christian faith with religion and its fate, and thus be able to regard it as a special case of religion, and Marxism persistently does. Admittedly Feuerbach and Marx's theory of religion is inadequate, but even its improvement and deepening in no way alters the fact that, as Feuerbach rightly saw, the mystery is not God but man. All apologetics on behalf of religion from Schleiermacher down to Toynbee, confirm this fact by seeking to demonstrate the inevitability and indispensability of religion for the schooling and unfolding of man. There is much truth in this, and just for this reason it is absolutely certain that the Marxist rationalism will never cease to be faced by the religions, and the insatiable character of the

need for religion. But it would be disastrous if we were to hope that by means of this demonstration and this discussion we could win some gain for the Christian faith, for

(*a*) Immanentism cannot be conquered by this means (or at best only in an idealistic manner, in terms of our need for transcendence, and this is no real conquest). Theology can have no interest in refuting immanentism in respect of religion. But it cannot prove, or wish to prove, that the living God to whom the biblical word bears witness does not belong to the immanent conditions of the world, and is not a product of our need. It can, however, indicate that this is not so, by showing how in his revelation he distinguishes himself from the gods. The criticism of the religions does not deny the existence of the gods, but allocates them to the world, to the one creaturely world. The biblical account of creation itself confirms the truth of immanentism—"Heaven and earth" (Genesis 1:1)—that is all, only this one homogeneous world, in contrast with the Creator, nothing but world. It is with the powers of this world, positive and negative, that we have to do in religion, not with the Creator himself, who must in his freedom encounter us, in order that we may have such dealings with him as to know him and be able to speak with him. Therefore the gospel does not take part or engage itself in the fight between the religious and the irreligious.

(*b*) This becomes especially important with the rise of a secularism of which Marxism itself is only one of the possible forms of expression. The non-religious man of the present does not require first to be led to religion, transformed into a religious man, in order then to take a second step along this way to come to the Christian faith. Without his putting himself in a religious frame of mind, creating for himself religious experiences, awakening within himself a so-called natural consciousness of God, thus without his being compelled to adopt forms of consciousness which he can no longer recapture, he must be encountered in his life, which has become secular, by the good news from the Lord of the world, who has committed himself in the man Jesus of Nazareth to the world and the secularity of the stable and the gallows ("without the camp" of religion, Hebrews 13:13!). We touch here upon Dietrich Bonhoeffer's problem of the "non-religious interpretation" of the Christian message, and can only just indicate the task which this problem has set us.

(c) The real antithesis which theology must insist on, is not that between religion and atheism, but between the "God for us" of the gospel, and the human refusal to live in the strength of the vital reality of this "God for us". This refusal, this mistrust by man of his divine Lord, this insistence on arranging his life by means of his own care and efforts, can take religious and profane, rational and mystical, technical and superstitious forms. The fronts, which today stand so sternly opposed to each other (including the so-called Christian fronts) are to a great extent nothing but competing fronts of self-redemption, each of them desiring to bind men to use its recipe, in order to dominate them. Their self-righteousness, their deadly enmity, their fanaticism, their tense unscrupulousness, their humourlessness, their unreadiness to repent are clear signs of the curse of the "law" under which they stand—"law" used here in the theological sense of the word; they are competitors within the one hopelessness and joylessness of the law. The activity which they know is not one which arises from the grateful reception of God's love, but a restless activity which stems from anxiety about a heavenly or earthly salvation, which must be earned by it. Therefore nothing is bettered by a conversion from atheism to religion, or from religion to atheism.[10] The only conversion which brings something new, is that from law to gospel. It does not stand in our power, but is the effect of the gospel itself in the power of a greater Spirit, whom we have not at our disposal, but who lets his work be proclaimed in the Christian message; it is called "faith" in the authentic,

[10] On the reciprocal rights of atheism and religion, cf. E. Brunner, *The Divine Imperative*, pp. 62ff.

Christian sense. This conversion ends our existence as functionaries of a front representing a world-view, and makes us messengers of the love which from above seeks every individual, the religious man as the atheist, as a creature beloved, which must leave the tense struggle against the feared non-being, to receive fellowship with him who places himself between the creature and non-being. The Christian community in the Communist society will be compelled to test its whole life to see whether it is a witness to, and a vivid picture of this evangelical "invitation to the godless".

(d) Thus it is possible without prejudice, without irritation, and defensiveness to discuss with the Marxists the phenomenon and the problems of religion. Not the Christian message but our human method of receiving and embodying it, the Christian religion, will there, so far as Christianity is in question, be dealt with, but it must not be withdrawn from criticism. In this, theology will be both the defender of religion over against the onesidedness, the superficiality and the fatuities of Marxist criticism, and at the same time the ally of this criticism against cruelties, stuffiness, terrorism and like inhumanities of the religious life.

5. Marxism roundly denies theology the possibility of ranking as a science.[11] If, none the less, it claims as a rational discipline dealing with the mystery of revelation, a claim to the title "science" and a legitimate place in the university, this means that by so doing it shares in responsibility for the life and nature of the sciences in general. This shows itself particularly in the fact that it does not make a monopolistic claim to that title, not as a polemical assertion, which would refuse this title to the other sciences. Theology indeed participates in the other sciences, has a nexus with them, uses them, welcomes them in its own sphere, inasmuch as here also, for

[11] With abundance of invective even before Feuerbach (P. Bayle, *Krönerausgabe,* pp. 19f., 32), by the young Engels ("Theology the Original Type of all other Lies and Hypocrisy", MEGA, I, 2, p. 426) by Marx (*Deutsche Ideologie,* pp. 241, 578); "Theology from the first the putrefying sore of philosophy (*Frühschriften,* p. 227).

example, philosophy and history in the strict sense are studied. It is certainly not really "a" science, but (in this resembling medicine), a sphere in which different sciences are united by their service of a determinate purpose, the critical self-examination of the Church in relation to the correspondence between its actual achievement and its task. Thus interwoven with the universal life of science, theology must justify the responsibility given thereby to it for this life by (1) not mis-leading the other sciences into unreality through dogmatic prejudices and restrictions, but by showing itself positively interested in a free investigation which is limited by no law save that of the knowledge of its subject, (2) by itself not fail-ing to develop methods suited to its special subject, and not failing in critical responsibility for its action, or in the effort to clarify its concepts, (3) by being, through its peculiar char-acter, a disturbing question in the scientific world, an indis-pensable indication of the limits of the possibilities of science.

This peculiarity consists in the fact that it is related to a history, the history of revelation, about which it must make statements which go beyond the appearances which are access-ible to the historian—that it has a text which stands in a quite different degree than do other texts under the dialect of "the letter and the spirit" and which, therefore, shows up the inadequacy of every exegetical method—that its history, as the history of the discipline concerned with such an extra-ordinary subject-matter, is a history more of failure than of success. For this reason it awakens, and not only among Marxists, the doubt whether one may here speak of a science, or whether one must not rather speak of the perversion of science. But the creation of unrest, the disturbance of fixed prejudices, is not a perversion, but a help. By reason of its unprotected character, by reason of its special problems of method, theology reminds us that every method as a special perspective bearing on an object, is for this very reason a limited perspective; it protests by its existence even more strongly than the mental sciences against the establishment of a concept of science which is merely copied from the model of the natural sciences; by its existence it fosters the self-critical freedom of science to acknowledge its own limits and provisional character. The freedom of science is not threatened —so long as it rightly understands itself—by theology, but principally by scientism, by the superstition which makes a world-view out of modern science, and uses it as a quarry for the building of world pictures allegedly demanded and authorized by science. The danger of science is the unsatisfied need for faith which, after the decay of other forms of faith, demands its satisfaction from science. Contrary to the opinion of Georg Klaus, that religion hinders the investigator in the consistent pursuit of his inquiries,[12] we can cite plenty of cases in the history of science, even of Soviet science, where an obstacle was created, not by religions, but by rationalistic, causalist, mechanist prejudices, not to speak of subjectivist pet ideas, vanities, and narrowmindedness. Every assumption, every hypothesis can in science grow into a prejudice. Rightly understood, theology opens the way unconditionally to every investigation of fact. Faith in the Creator is actually an affirmation of things as they are, and is opposed to all well-meaning misrepresentation or taboo. Where science is understood as in conflict with faith (in the biblical sense of the word), and as a substitute for religion, the place is necessarily assigned to it religion previously occupied. It is then required to give what it cannot give. It is then neither free nor subject to criticism, it becomes itself a taboo. Science must prove its freedom also in this, that it recognizes itself as a specific and therefore limited mode of knowledge, to which other aspects of reality are closed, e.g. in the sphere of nature, modes of knowledge of a non-rational and non-experimental kind, such as are used in other cultures, and such as are brought to our

[12] *Jesuiten, Gott, Materie,* pp. 85, 87f., 166, 248. On this subject Erich Vögelin is useful to read, though vitiated by ill-temper: "Wissenschaft als Aberglaube" in *Wort und Wahreit,* 1951/5, pp. 341-60, and the observations of K. Jaspers (*Der Monat,* 1950/26, p. 143) and K. A. Wittvogel, "Theoretische Ketzereien" in *Ostprobleme,* 1954/4.

knowledge today in the anthroposophical conception of nature. Only scientific dogmatism can argue that these methods are condemned by the fact that for us today no synthesis of these other forms by our modern Western methods is yet possible. The scientific attitude is not incompatible with Christian faith, but with the superstitious faith in science, and with the subjection of science to the demands of a need to believe, which finds an ideological satisfaction in it.

6. The explanation of the world serves both self-mastery and the attainment of security of existence, the *discovery of meaning*. The ancient Christian metaphysic was theological, not only because it had recourse to God for the explanation of world-phenomena, but also because it regarded the basis of its explanations as identical with the basis and goal which gives meaning to the world. Marxism equally turns the scientific explanation of the world into theology, by claiming to draw from it the material for an answer to the question of meaning. What dangers this implies for science have been just stated, now we must ask what reflections theology must have in relation to this kind of answer to the question of meaning.

In an earlier section reference was made to the secret resignation which is concealed in this answer, and consequently to its inadequate and not genuinely satisfactory character. I do not mean by this that Marxism has been playing with a false pack of cards. Its promise was to give an answer under the conditions of modern thought, i.e. the best possible answer under the conditions of a world left to itself, the prospect of ourselves giving a relative meaning to a meaningless world. When Paul Tillich in a conversation once said, in my opinion, most illuminatingly, that today there are only Stoics and Christians, then Marxism is a kind of positive Stoicism; more meaning is unfortunately not our lot, but at least we have this much! In Marxism—but of course not in it alone—the man of the modern age, the secular world, sees himself condemned to the destiny (or as we shall also have at once to formulate it; he wills the destiny)—of self-sufficiency

160

both in the matter of explaining the world, and in respect of the question of meaning.

On the Christian side we must not at once triumphantly assert that this cannot succeed. Nor were our earlier arguments meant to lead to such a premature conclusion; for in order to understand them it must be noted that the standard by which measurement was there made was the promise of meaning given by the Christian gospel. What it means to apply this standard, that is a question which theology must clarify for itself, as a task of reflection which will serve the proclamation of the Christian gospel in a Communist environment. The inadequacy of the Communist answer cannot be demonstrated within the Communist context. It fulfils just as much as it promises in the first instance—and how is man to know that "rationally"—as Feuerbach is accustomed to say in such a connection[13]—he must not be content with these limitations as with so many others. Indeed the resignation which is bound up with it, the urgent longing and desire for a better, more satisfying answer, which finds expression in the religious production, is a striking sign which should give even the rationalist food for thought—but where there is nothing, the Emperor has lost his rights, and it is wisdom that teaches us that resignation is not to be considered a merely negative thing, for when we turn to the community, and seek the desired meaning in service to it, then the metaphysical disappointment has after all borne positive fruit.

The realization that this is a makeshift, in contrast with which the disillusionment with its distress expresses a truth —can be suppressed. It must be suppressed, so long as nothing else offers. That in this self-sufficiency man hungers, and starves to death, is the biblical judgment upon it. But is this demonstrable? That would presuppose an objective standard of peace and fulfilment, by which one could assess the minimum for existence which a world-view must guarantee. There is no such standard. Marxism itself teaches the historical

[13] Cf. the 22nd Lecture on the Nature of Religion.

conditioning of human needs, although on the other hand it can speak of them as timeless ascertainable entities. In contrast with physical needs it must be said of spiritual ones that we only come to know them in our encounters. Those children, of whom it is told that the Hohenstaufen King Friedrich II caused them to be brought up for an experiment without conversation, caresses, or laughter, did not know what they lacked, but they perished for the lack of it. How inadequate an answer is, how much it remains below the "minimum for existence" is only evident in the light of the full answer. What life and meaning can really mean, is only shown in an encounter which gives these words a new and more excellent meaning. What man "needs" for life cannot be ascertained apart from this. It is only the new encounter which creates a standard for the rest. It is only the new encounter which really awakens the question which it answers. It so radicalizes it that now the hunger is intolerable. Thus it is not the case that the fullness of meaning experienced in the gospel is the answer to an already manifest question. What the gospel offers is the answering of a question and the fulfilment of a need which is only awakened by the gospel. Therefore it can be satisfied only by the gospel. We are thus confronted here by a circle which we are always coming up against when we concern ourselves with theology; the gospel is the answer to a life-question; relevant, fully satisfying answer, but the question only arises through the proclamation of the answer. This circle can at first give the whole matter the appearance of capriciousness, as if a need were brought to man, or suggested to him, which was not previously and spontaneously and naturally his need. But it is not so. It is to be noted that our problem is one in the noetic sphere, the sphere of what man knows his need to be, not of what his need is. What in the light of the gospel he recognizes as need, lack and hunger, he suffered from already. But now he is aware of it, as a man who through illness has lost the pain that is the indication of the wound, only feels it when he is

162

cured of the loss of sensation. The connection between his knowledge now and his real previous condition is made clear by the fact that the pain is the pain of the wound which was previously visible, but seemed tolerable and not deadly, and which only now receives its right interpretation through the pain. So the death-bringing lack of fellowship with God, and the devastation wrought by evil is visible before the encounter with God's condescension in the gospel, in all the phenomena of estrangement, lack of fellowship, perversion of life, which cause the ever-repeated attempts to heal life, the religious as well as the atheistic ones. But how deep the injury is, and how inadequate, indeed, how destined to lead to further evil are the remedies offered for healing, this is only evident when God himself comes on the scene and his appearing at once judges our previous state as our own self-inflicted misery and removes it. Only in concrete encounter with the Word of God that speaks to us does man's destiny become clear, and only in the light of this highest destiny of life in fellowship with God is the previous condition unmasked as the misery of the man who has forfeited his high destiny, and the also previously visible signs of defect and wickednesses of life are exposed as consequences of forfeiting his destiny. The destiny, or, as we earlier said, the promise of the gospel—namely the restoration and realization of the destiny of man, is now the standard by which all other remedies are measured. When this is done, it becomes clear that they all lie within the limits of the loss of the true destiny of life, and are therefore inadequate, being themselves only an expression of this loss. This standard comes from nothing less than the resurrection of the dead. Therefore H. J. Iwand who, with special consistence in our times, has expounded the Christian message as message of the resurrection of the dead, said once in comment on the remarkable word of the apostle Paul, "If in this life only we have hope in Christ, we are of all men most miserable" (I Cor. 15:19): "When Paul confronts the power of the living God with the power of death, by relating these two, God and death, without any mediating terms . . . he reaches the final most extreme position in order to proclaim the gospel of Jesus Christ as the victory of God along the whole line. From the far side of death, from outside of the history of man, which is determined by death, stems the message of Christ. If it does not remain inseparably bound with the other, with the inconceivable reality of the resurrection of the dead as the crossing of the boundaries of this age and its laws, then it is meaningless, then our Christianity, with all that belongs to it, with the forgiveness of sins and immortality is nothing more than one of the many 'religions of redemption', then as today so numerous, with which the prisoners console themselves about the inviolability of their prison.''[14]

In these remarks we have described one of the results of the discussions concerning the problem of so-called natural theology which have agitated Protestant theology in the last decades.[15] It has significance in our context, because it is part of the theological task in the conversation between Marxism and Christian faith to make clear the origin of the standard by which the fulfilment of human history claimed by Communism is measured in the moment when it not only aims at bringing the greatest possible improvement in the life of society, but enters as a Messianic promise into competition with the Christian promise, in order to make the latter superfluous.

The standard is thus neither merely that of scepticism, which regards the goal as too ambitiously formulated, nor one which without further question is visible to our partner, because he on his side regards such a standard as too ambitiously formulated, as fantastic. So he will at once con-

[14] In a Meditation on I Corinthians 15 in G. Eichholz's *Herr, tue, meine Lippen auf,* Wuppertal 1955, 4th vol., p. 257.
[15] An acute exposure of natural theology with the proof that it is only concerned with man's attempts at finding his own security is given by Marx in his criticism of Plutarch, "Vorarbeiten zur Dissertation" in MEGA, I, 1, i, pp. 111f. Cf. the account by Bockmühl, op. cit. pp. 116f.

164

cede that in the light of such a standard his position, enthusi-astic as it may seem to the sceptic, is a position of resignation, but it is just this which he will consider reasonable and realistic. At this point is shown the difficulty of the Christian proclamation in an environment in which it can no longer assume the presence of "metaphysical needs", which them-selves were probably a deposit of centuries of Christian preaching. The Church finds itself in a very alien environ-ment, not only when confronting conscious Marxists, but also in the midst of the masses of the people influenced by them, and often looks round vainly for "points of contact", for common standards, with whose help it can demonstrate that only the gospel does not give a stone instead of bread. In this situation it is a protection against ineffective tactics, and against disappointments and depressions, if there is theo-logical clarity about the fundamental strangeness, novelty, and undemonstrability of the gospel promises. The Church in this situation is thrown entirely upon its faith in the self-evidencing power of its message—not as if it were now per-mitted to speak in the alien language of Canaan, not as if it were permitted to neglect a careful endeavour to use language which closely touches the real experience of the hearer, and is intelligible to him, and the search for all possible oppor-tunities of making contact. But it must understand clearly that with this effort of its own to serve, it will not overcome the strangeness and the lack of comprehension unless the word to which it bears witness itself becomes the encounter which creates new dimensions of understanding and need. It can-not demonstrate to blind eyes, so that these will then be opened by a free decision; it can only proclaim to blind eyes the message committed to it, in the hope that this call itself, and he who is proclaimed in it as the real one will open men's eyes to the real life and provide the real standard, as he must do also in the case of the preachers, the Christians, them-selves daily. In the estrangement which Communism creates by its destruction of Christian traditions among the people, it is a reinforcement of the confidence of the Christian witness in face of daily discouragements, to understand clearly that fundamentally the situation was always like this, and that this is part of the essential peculiarity of the gospel; the proclamation of this message cannot be made in any other way than by presupposing what is only created by itself, than by appealing to a desire which it must not vainly expect to find awaiting it, but which it only creates by the event of its own proclamation. Not the "old" man, but only the "new" man, the man who is touched by the approach of the living God, will regard every other promise as arrogant, and every offered substitute as profoundly inadequate.

If the props which it previously used are thus struck away from the Christian proclamation, because Marxism asserts that it is not necessary, either to explain the world, or to heal the ills of humanity, so it must, with all the more confidence, put its own message into words, without anxiety about the strangeness to which we have referred. It must do this even for the sake of Communism, which continally over-reaches itself with its own promises, and therefore reels from one disappointment to another, instead of limiting and concentrating itself on what it can achieve. It must do this for the sake of men, who have to suffer the consequences of this promise, which aims too high, and therefore not high enough, and can indeed for a time conceal the abyss of despair and cynicism and hollow resignation, but cannot really exorcise its attractive power.

There are two further reasons why precisely in the discussion with Marxism it is positively and specially important that theology should make clear to itself how the Christian message cannot demonstrate the indispensability and superiority of its promise by reference to the reality as it is accessible to man before his eyes are opened by the gospel.

(a) Were this possible, it would confirm the mistrust that runs through the Marxist criticism of religion, that this message may be nothing but a product of need, created for the purpose of satisfying it. That God is the means to an end, even if an ineffective one, is a point in which Feuerbach and Marx are at one. How far this construction from a preceding need and consequent religious ideas goes towards explaining the phenomena of the history of religion, is a question which may here be left undecided.

But at least we can say that this schema breaks down as an attempt to explain the origin of the biblical message about God. Here the possibility does not precede the reality, the need does not precede its satisfaction, but the reality creates the new possibilities, the needs, *and* their appeasement. God is not a means valued by man—who, for example, could harmonize such an idea with the prophetic challenges in the Old Testament!—but before all value, before what he can signify for human life, he is Himself. Feuerbach's theory of religion with its schema of needs, converts the Bible into a philosophy of value, which from the start falsifies its content. That human ideas can contain something other than value judgments, is a thought strange to this subjectivism. Anyone who wishes adequately to understand biblical texts must free himself from it, and understand that there are encounters which primarily have their significance as such, and in relation to which the consideration of value is only secondary. Personal encounter is of this kind. Where the purpose of a fellowship stands in the foreground, it loses its power of reality. This is supremely true of the biblical encounter with God; whether it brings life or death is not the first question, God is primarily subject, and as subject important, as the one who He is, and only secondarily because of his "predicates", i.e. because of the values which we conjoin with the thought of God. Because Feuerbach judged as an outsider, it was not possible for him to grasp this, and the question of value thrust itself upon him. Therefore in order rightly to understand our discussion, it is necessary to emphasize how it is not meant in the sense of such a value concept as Feuerbach's. It should show that the Communist promise cannot compare as a serious competitor with the standard of the Christian promise. But it does not aim to prove the truth of the Christian promise by reason of its value; it does not aim to recommend God because one can't get on without him. Its aim is not to plead for God by means of the human need for meaning. All this is true; this promise is superior and satisfying; it holds good where everything else fails, it gives purchase and meaning, and God is the one no one can get on without. But all this is true because before all God is God, i.e. not a means to such ends, but an end in himself, and therefore not a means to life for man, alongside of whom one might conjecture there were other means, but life itself. It is not man and his needs that can be the meaning of God's existence, but God is the meaning of the existence of man. Therefore what man receives in the encounter with God is not visible outside of or before this encounter, not outside of "faith". For only in this encounter does God himself become important to men, not because of his meaning, or any value, but He himself—and just this is the most supremely satisfying answer to the question of meaning.

(b) In the second place this discussion is important because it shows that in the conversation between Christian faith and Marxist atheism, affirmations and denials do not meet each other. What the atheist denies is not what the Christian affirms. The difference of interpretation seems insuperable, which reminds us that even in other cases, a miracle happens when men understand each other, i.e. when the same contents communicate themselves in the same words. The whole polemic of Feuerbach indicates that the Christian faith is interpreted as the "assumption" of the existence of a God, as the hypothesis that there is such an existence, and only distinguishes itself from polytheism by its concentration on one instead of many. The triumph over the fact that the sputnik and the subsequent space-travellers discovered no such being in the world of space is only an element of bathos in anti-religious propaganda and a booby-trap. The possibility of such primitive argumentation is, however, based on the fact that the denial of God occurs on the same ontological level as that on which people can discuss the existence of Martians; here one can set up theories pro and con; here one can some day by testing discover who is right. To discuss in this manner, on this plane, about "God" in the sense in which the Christian faith uses the word and confesses the reality of God, is about as inadequate as if one were to deal with the question of the freedom of the will on the anatomical plane. The denial which finds expression in the assertion that "there is no God" believes it is speaking about the Christian God, but speaks about something quite different. Karl Barth therefore rightly said—strangely causing many theologians to shake their heads anxiously—that the arguments of Marxist atheism did not deal with the God of the Christian confession, but a "conceptual idol", and that it was an important task of the Christians in conversation with the Marxists to deny his identity with the God of faith.[16] In the same sense Dietrich Bonhoeffer wrote as early as 1930, "A God who 'exists' does not exist".[17] About the same time Hans J. Iwand formulated theses about "Faith and Scepticism", of which some were as follows:[18]

"9. Just as certainly as man can doubt the grace of God, so little can he doubt the existence of God.

"10. God's being cannot therefore be denied because it would have to be conceived in order to be possible of denial.

"12. It cannot be proved that God is, but is can be proved that the sentence 'God is not' is senseless."

The sentence "God is not" is senseless because it claims to be a denial of an existence within the world, which it is possible therefore to deny. In this way we can deny the existence of the gods. But if this sentence refers to the God

[16] *Brief an einen Pfarrer in der D.D.R.*, 1958, pp. 19f.
[17] *Act and Being*, p. 126.
[18] Now in *Glauben und Wissen*, Munich 1961, p. 278.

of Christian faith, it betrays that the man who says it has no idea of what he is speaking about, that he is the victim of a confusion—or, on whatever grounds—is insisting on a confusion. If he knew what he was speaking about, he would also know that he can well doubt whether the one before whom he here stands, signifies life or death to him, that he can well doubt his grace; for if he knows of whom he is speaking, he speaks as one who stands before him: "Thou hast beset me behind and before, and laid thine hand upon me" (Psalm 139:5). Thus he does not know, that in denying God's existence, he is not expressing an uncommitted judgment, not making an objective statement of fact, but saying "No" to the living God: i.e. denying his own existence. Thus he does not know—precisely like the men who put Jesus on the cross—what he is doing. He does not know that the word "God", when he means that word in the Christian sense, reaches a plane where it is not a case of ascertaining existent facts, but where a judgment is passed on his own existence. I make judgments about existent facts without thereby altering myself. But the denial of God cannot at all be spoken in this way as a meaningful sentence; the sentence "God is not" is either thoughtless chatter, or it is a self-cancellation in revolt; "God must not be". It is only possible so long as I believe that I can pass a judgment about a something which is customarily called "God", and thus do not realize that the Christian faith, when it speaks of God, does not express a judgment about a something, but tells of him who utters a judgment on all of us, who is too high for our judgment. For this reason Karl Barth wrote (about the same time as Iwand's theses) in his book on Anselm:[19] "The man who negates God's being, must allow himself to be asked if he is really thinking of *him quo majus cogitari nequit.*[20] If he

---

[19] *Fides Quaerens Intellectum Anselms, Beweis der Existenz Gottes*, Munich, 1930, p. 167.

[20] "He than whom no higher can be conceived", this is the description of God in Anselm's proof.

170

is not thinking of him, then he is obviously not denying *his* being. If he is thinking of him, then he is thinking of the one whose being cannot be denied."

At this point at the end of the whole study, the subject which has so long occupied us seems to be dissolving into cloud. What is this atheism in reality? Obviously a denial that is quite impossible, that is an impossible possibility. This one can only make so long as one does not know what one is doing. Obviously a sentence which in itself is meaningless, if we understand by that a sentence in which subject and predicate cannot be denied because the subject in its being cannot be the subject of this predicate, and the predicate in its being cannot be the predicate of this subject—a sentence consequently which is only grammatically but not logically possible. It is good and meaningful that at the end atheism turns out to be such an enigmatic structure—not as something unintelligible—no, it is only too intelligible to us all—but as an assertion, whose meaning is lost in an impenetrable haze.

For the Christian who sees himself outwardly and inwardly oppressed by the atheistic denial, this should be an indication of the fact that atheism is really, according to the well-known word of Heinrich Vogel, *vanitas vanitatum*, by whose power and craft we should not let ourselves be impressed. At the same time the analysis of what can underlie the sentence "God, this God, the living God! is not"—thoughtless chatter or suicidal revolt—shows that the sentence itself gives no confirmation on the point. Thus we cannot tell from the atheistic assertion what event we have before us. The Christian answer can therefore in no case be an anticipation of the last judgment, for the Christian only sees what is before his eyes, hears only what is before his ears, a sentence which cannot touch or obliterate the one to whom he, the Christian, is bound to bear witness, but perhaps touches the one to whom he has actually referred, a conceptual idol who is rightly touched by such a denial. So the Christian answer will have to be accompanied by a self-critical examination of one's own

171

previous statements. At this point also we come to the conclusion that in no case must indignation influence this answer because, even where we have not to deal with thoughtless confusion, but with rebellion against God's claim, only pity is in place, and a self-critical question as to how far one has shared oneself in guilt by being a bad witness to the reality of God.

All the more does the grace of the task given us in the midst of the conflict of "Yes" and "No" become evident; Communism extols itself not only as a revolutionary movement of reform, as which it can and must be a matter for discussion. It extols itself as "the solution of the riddle of human history".[21] By so doing it extols human action as the solution of the human riddle. The gospel, on the other hand, gives us the motive actively to confront human needs by regarding the solution of the riddle itself as in other hands. It shows as the agent one who succeeds in finding the solution, not the revolutionary fighter with an allegedly omnipotent theory. It announces the hour in which the book of riddles of history still lies there sealed with seven seals, and to the question who is worthy to open it and to loose the seals, the fighters and the wise men, the theoreticians and the men of action are all silent. "And no man in heaven, nor in earth, neither under the earth, was able to open the book, neither to look thereon." But while hopeless weeping about this goes through the universe, a Lamb as it had been slain takes the book—and already the answer to the question about the solution is secured and in the whole universe thankful jubilation replaces the weeping of despair (Rev. 5). The Christian Church is

[21] So Marx, cf. p. 71 with a similar statement of Engels, "Die Lage Englands" in *Nachlass*, vol. I, p. 486f: "Man has only himself to know, he must measure all the conditions of life by himself, estimate them by his own standards, judge them by his nature, organize the world according to the demands of his nature in a truly human fashion, and he has solved the riddle of our times. Not in transcendent non-existent regions, not beyond time and space, not with 'God' dwelling in the world or set over against it, is the truth to be found, but rather in man's own breast".

placed in this universe, which agonizes about a solution, as witness to the acts of God, by which the redemption is already secured. Therefore it can confess the reality of God. For "He only knows about God who is the witness—however distant and humble—to his action. And he speaks of God, and only he who—however faultily—can give a report of his action".[22] This act discloses man as the beloved creature, the world not as nature, giving birth to itself to eternity, solitary and meaningless, but as the creation, which praises its Creator; this act is, as the grasp of the Creator upon his humanity, that misunderstands him, forsakes him, and therefore also denies its own nature, the true solution of its riddle: "Every philosophical contradiction, and the whole historical riddle of our existence, the impenetrable might of its *termini a quo* and *termini ad quem*, is solved by the charter of the incarnate Word."[23]

[22] K. Barth, *Church Dogmatics*, Edinburgh, 1961, IV, i, p. 7.

[23] Johann Georg Hamann (Selections by Arnold, 1888, p. 162). For the interpretation of the young Marx the recently published book of H. Rohr, *Pseudoreligiöse Motive in den Frühschriften von Karl Marx*, Tübingen, 1962, unfortunately makes no useful contribution. His own contribution to scholarship consists simply of a polemic against all attempts to find in Marx traces of the influence of biblical, Jewish and Christian thinking. He asserts in opposition to this, that Marx only wished to offer "pure philosophy"—a fact which was not unknown to those whom he attacks. For the concept of political Messianism and its fate in modern times see the discussion following on a contribution by J. L. Talmon at the Seminary of Rheinfelden, "Die Industrielle Gesellschaft und die drei Welten" in *Das Seminar von Rheinfelden*, Zürich, 1961, pp. 199–222. A development of the view here expounded, especially of Chapters VI to VIII, is to be found in two other essays of the author, now both printed in my volume of essays, *Forderungen der Freiheit. Aufsätze und Reden zur politischen Ethik*, Munich, 1962, pp. 211–20 and pp. 191–211.